D1752554

Front cover:
The Rayol estate

Routes of Discovery

FRENCH RIVIERA

TEXT
SIMONETTA GREGGIO

PHOTOGRAPHS
GRÉGOIRE GOSSET

TRANSLATION : ENTREPRISES 35

Éditions Ouest-France

CONTENTS

Map of the French riviera **6**

Introduction **9**

The myth of the French riviera **11**

Discovering the Riviera's gardens **33**

Tastes of the French Riviera **53**

Perched villages **69**

The islands **97**

Bibliography **121**

Recommended addresses **123**

Map of Provence region

Map showing the Provence-Alpes-Côte d'Azur region of southeastern France, with inset map of France highlighting the region.

Key locations shown:

Départements / Regions:
- VAUCLUSE 84
- BOUCHES-DU-RHÔNE (13)
- VAR (83)
- PROVENCE
- TRÉVARESSE
- SAINTE-VICTOIRE
- CHAÎNE DE L'ÉTOILE
- CHAÎNE DE LA STE-BAUME
- PARC DU VERDON
- GRAND PLAN DE CANJUERS

Water features:
- Durance
- Verdon
- Argens
- Lac du Barrage de Ste-Croix
- Étang de Berre

Cities and towns:
- Marseille
- Aix-en-Provence
- Toulon
- Hyères
- Rognac
- Vitrolles
- Marignane
- Châteauneuf-les-Martigues
- Cabriès
- Gardanne
- Bouc-Bel-Air
- Allauch
- Roquevaire
- Auriol
- Trets
- St-Maximin-la-Ste-Baume
- Plan-d'Aups-Ste-Baume
- Nans-les-Pins
- Gémenos
- Aubagne
- La Penne-sur-Huveaune
- Carnoux-en-Provence
- Cassis
- La Ciotat
- St-Cyr-sur-Mer
- Bandol
- Sanary-sur-Mer
- La Seyne-sur-Mer
- Six-Fours-les-Plages
- St-Mandrier-sur-Mer
- Le Beausset
- Ollioules
- La Farlède
- La Valette-du-Var
- La Garde
- La Grau
- Le Pradet
- Carqueiranne
- Giens
- La Tour-Fondue
- Signes
- Tourves
- La Roquebrussanne
- Brignoles
- Besse-sur-Issole
- Le Luc
- Cuers
- Pierrefeu-du-Var
- Solliès-Pont
- Collobrières
- La Londe-les-Maures
- Bormes-les-Mimosas
- Le Lavandou
- Rians
- Tavernes
- Barjols
- Cotignac
- Aups
- Salernes
- Flayosc
- Lorgues
- Senez
- Moustiers-Ste-Marie

Mountain:
- ▲ 1041 Bertagne

Islands:
- Presqu'île de Giens
- Cap Sicié
- Porquerolles
- Île de Porquerolles
- Île de Port-Cros

Major roads: A7, A8, A51, A52, A50, A55, A57, A570

Scale: 0 — 3 km

PARC NATIONAL DU MERCANTOUR
ALPES
ALPES-MARITIMES
06
ITALIE
PRINCIPAUTÉ DE MONACO
CHEIRON
ESTÉREL
CÔTE D'AZUR
MER MÉDITERRANÉE
3143 Cime du Gélas
Col de Tende 1279
Tende
Valberg
St-Sauveur-sur-Tinée
Guillaumes
Beuil
St-Martin-Vésubie
Roquebillière
Lantosque
Tinée
Var
Puget-Théniers
Entrevaux
Villars-sur-Var
Annot
Peïra-Cava
Breil-sur-Roya
Sospel
Lac de Castillon
Castellane
St-Auban
Roquesteron
Levens
Carros
Contes
L'Escarène
San Remo
Menton
Ventimiglia
Bordighera
Coursegoules
La Trinité
La Turbie
Roquebrune-Cap-Martin
Beausoleil
Monte-Carlo
Monaco
La Gaude
Vence
Nice
Èze
A8
Gourdon
La Colle-sur-Loup
1715 Mt de Lachens
Le Bar-sur-Loup
St-Paul
Beaulieu-sur-Mer
Villefranche-sur-Mer
St-Vallier-de-Thiey
Villeneuve-Loubet
St-Laurent-du-Var
Grasse
Cagnes-sur-Mer
Biot
Valbonne
Peymeinade
Fayence
Mougins
Antibes
Juan-les-Pins
Le Cannet
Lac de St-Cassien
Mandelieu-la-Napoule
Vallauris
Cannes
Cap d'Antibes
La Napoule
Théoule-s.-Mer
Îles de Lérins
Le Muy
LeTrayas
Puget-sur-Argens
Fréjus
Agay
St-Raphaël
Argens
Roquebrune-sur-Argens
St-Aygulf
La Garde-Freinet
Ste-Maxime
St-Tropez
Cap de St-Tropez
Cogolin
Cavalaire-sur-Mer
Le Canadel
Île du Levant

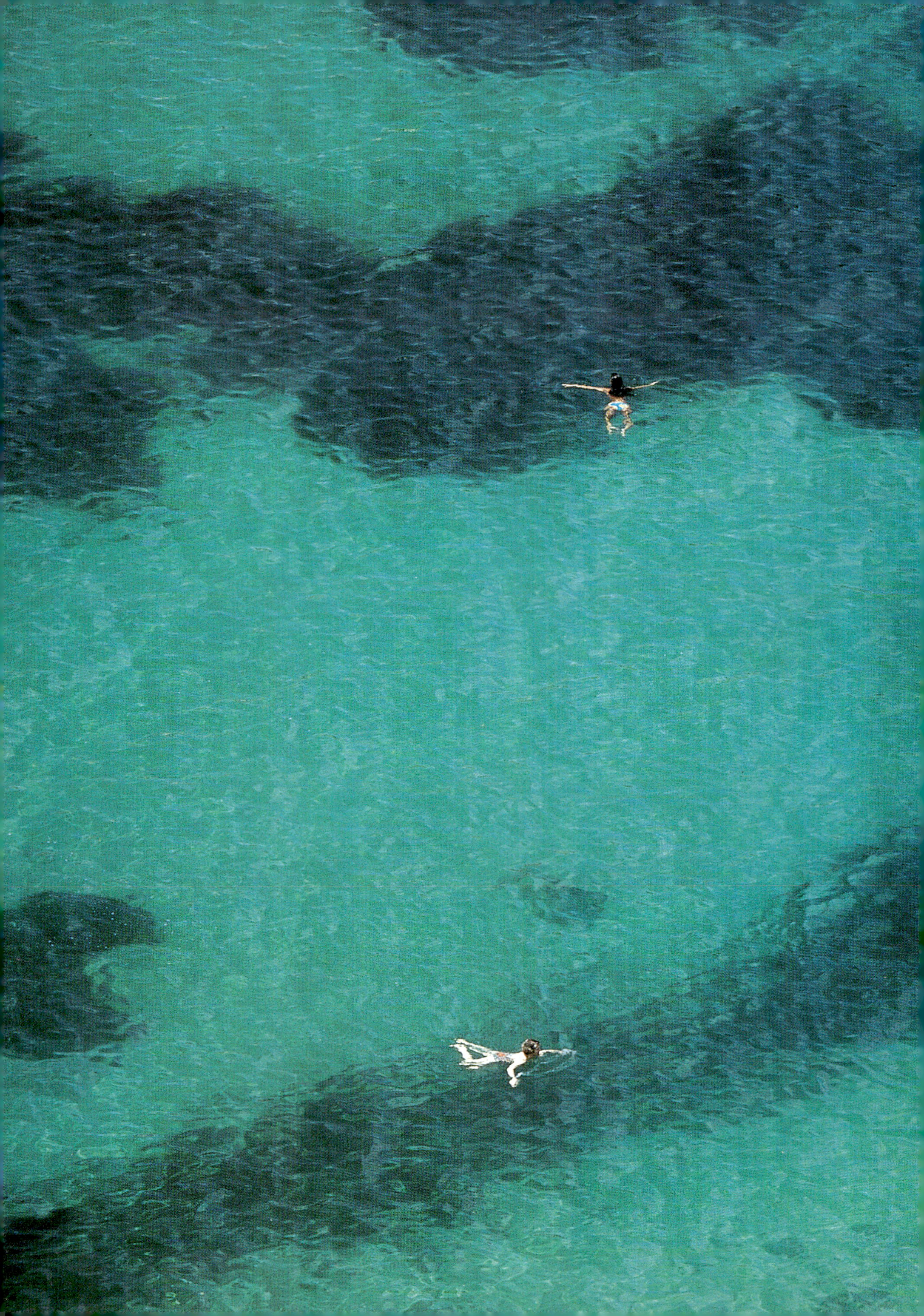

Introduction

"Well, my dear friend, you know how things are… Waking up, then work, a meal, some idle chatter, work again, another meal and then to bed. Hours go by, days go by, you get used to things, leading an exquisite life, but one with room for nothing more than the main essentials." (Roger Martin du Gard, in a letter to Gide, written in Cabris on November 21st, 1950).

The pages of my book about the French Riviera are stuck together with seawater. When at last I manage to separate them, a few grains of sand fall out.

In my book, there is my own French Riviera, the one I imagined when reading Scott Fitzgerald and Françoise Sagan, Conrad and Cyril Connolly, the one I still believe in even if at time it is obscured by "horrible apartment buildings" or hiding between coves with bits of plastic floating in them. I believe in the Riviera of my winter dreams in which I fall asleep to the soft sound of crickets and of waves lapping on warm sand dunes, when outside, "for real", it is cold and raining.

My book on the Riviera is full of all the things I read as a teenager, devouring the pages to the sound of a foxtrot on a terrace by the sea, Rosemary and Dick gazing into each others' eyes, Nicole flirting with Tommy, disappointment and weariness combined, children playing on a deserted beach under the watchful eye of their nanny at the end of that legendary spring. Scott Fitzgerald excelled at these rather ambivalent descriptions, caught as he was in the spider's web of his fame by a slowly declining style and indeed by fate itself.

For me, the French Riviera is that moonless night, lit only by the stars shining ever so brightly over the Esterel, when the beautiful, elegant Anne of "Bonjour Tristesse" drives her car off the top of the cliff.

My French Riviera misleads you as it did Gilles, who rented a little house in the Maures, home to his own solitary inner struggle. "Loners are rich with the admission of the true human situation."

Like Gilles, the unbearable yet charming Drieu La Rochelle believed for a while that here he would recover all the softness he had once found in women and in the sea.

The Riviera that I love and fear at the same time is the fresh, merciless and unbearably blue Riviera of Katherine Mansfield gasping for just enough breath to write one more page, one more book, to live one more day, knowing that each day was precious and each night numbered.

The superb Colette, or "Macolette" as her friend Marguerite Moreno called her, had her own approach to the French Riviera, with her young, tanned and beautiful friends, her cats and her early morning swims. She went barefoot, just as later BB, that other superb though very different woman, would do the same.

For me, when I think of the French Riviera, I think of my own youthful melancholy in the heavenly setting of the perched village of Eze, and then again of the hopes that I lost one day in that same heavenly setting.

Isn't it strange how at different times in your life the same view can be the setting for those deep feelings that mark you forever?

Isn't it strange how a swallow, swooping alone in a clear blue sky, can at times be a bad omen and at other times a good one?

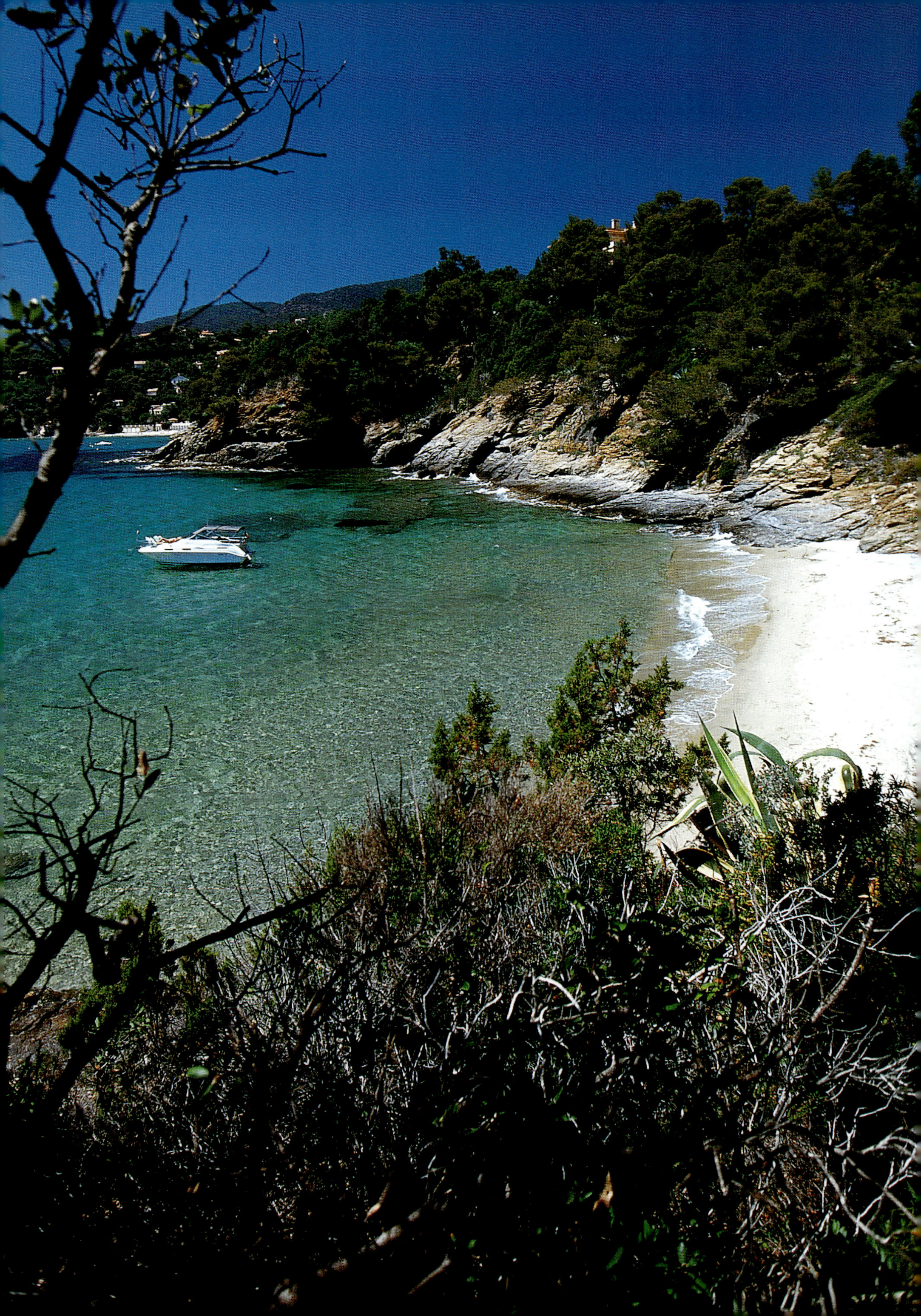

The myth
of the French Riviera

Menton
Monaco
Cap d'Ail
Beaulieu
Villefranche
Saint-Jean-Cap-Ferrat
Nice
Antibes
Le Cap d'Antibes
Juan-les-Pins
Cannes
Saint-Tropez

In 1887, Stephen Liégeard invented the name "Côte d'Azur". It was an inspired moment, since until then these two words which we now use so unthinkingly had never been used together. An azure coast with blue tinted waves, a touch of paradise where the lapis lazuli sky meets the Mediterranean Sea. This is what Liégeard sought to express in such a few, diffident words. How unfortunate that copyright procedures were not as efficient then as they are today - for generations to come, Mr Liégeard's descendants would have been free from all financial worries!

In a later edition of his book he notes: "The precise or outdated names for the Mediterranean coast - corniche, Riviera, Ligurian beaches - melted away like snow in the sun, leaving an empty space that was duly filled by briefer, more evocative terms that tended more towards reality than to poetry: the Côte d'Azur! From then on, this is how that land of blue sea, sun and flowers was to be known, from the Château d'If to the Palace of Genoa... A new word had been added to the dictionary."

At that time, the Riviera stretched all the way from Marseilles to Genoa, whereas today it runs only from Hyères to Menton, and does not include Cassis or Bandol. The old Riviera was as brief as it was intense, a kind of golden dream, tinted with the striking blue of campanula and morning glory, though ugly at times. Despite having succumbed to the concrete invasion of the 60s and 70s, the scent of jasmine still survives along the coastline.

"The sea forms a very blue bay. Kelp and old shoes on the beach. I love these mediocre places that do not torment the spectator." This is what Cocteau wrote to his mother from Carqueiranne in the spring of 1921, describing it as "the most ugly and the most endearing place in the world". Unfortunately, this description could apply to many of the beaches and bays of the Riviera, but by just pushing on for just a few kilometres to another view point, one is once again gazing wide-eyed at the classical beauty and lyricism of the Mediterranean.

In 1860, there were about one thousand French and foreign families wintering on the French Riviera, but it

Left:
The Rayol gardens. This is how the Riviera used to be, and still is at times.

How girls used to dress in the region: a flat hat and sailor suit.
(Coll. M. Sclaresky)

11

FRENCH RIVIERA

was not until 1931 that the hotels first opened their doors during the summer season.

Menton: perfect, secret, peaceful and forgotten, with its mild climate and irresistibly romantic gardens.

Nice, with the Cours Saleya, its flowers and cafes, balconies and ochre facades.

Saint-Tropez, swamped by too many admirers, and returning to normal in the autumn and spring months.

Cannes and its stars, Monaco and its casinos, abandoned rococo villas on the hillsides, and other jealously guarded villas built to house the wealth of the *nouveaux riches*. Exquisite islands lie at arm's reach, gleaming purple in the midday sun. Picasso, Cocteau, Paul Eluard and André Breton, beautiful black and white muses sitting at café terraces, with nothing more than a first name, Nusch or Tigy, to describe their silent beauty.

The Italian Riviera is just around the corner from Menton.

MENTON

With its gentle climate (one of the mildest in Europe), its exceptional location and peaceful lifestyle, Menton is one of the most attractive towns on the French Riviera. The vegetation is astounding. A riot of lemon, orange, and palm trees line the coast, whilst the rest of the town stretches up through olive trees on the hillsides.

The town has conserved an irresistible charm in the blue tint of its sun-bleached walls, climbing jasmine on yellow and gold facades, romantic balconies rusted by the sea air, and old fashioned promenades still echoing with the footsteps of all those young people who came here last century, hoping to recover their health.

"Some English tourists visiting the old cemetery in Menton, perched on terraces along the crest of the hill overlooking the town (in the 19th century it was known as 'the castle of the dead'), asked their guide why so many

FRENCH RIVIERA

young people were buried there. What battle was this? The answer is tuberculosis." ("La Côte d'Azur des écrivains", Edisud).

"Never a coffin in the street, no mourning cloth or funeral bells. That gaunt-looking person you saw out walking yesterday simply stops passing by your window, and that's it." (Maupassant, "Sur l'eau de Saint-Tropez à Monte-Carlo").

Katherine Mansfield and Nietzsche both came to this clement coastal town looking for a few moments of happiness in which to catch their breath. They did not die here, merely stopping to rest in Menton, seeking relief from their torment.

Today, the town remains unchanged, calm as ever, with a timeless feel to it. Italy is just a stone's throw away, beckoning you to discover its charms.

Menton is home to some of the most poetic gardens of the French Riviera, which are well worth a visit. It is even worth venturing across the border to enjoy the delicate yet grand Mortola gardens (see "Discovering the Riviera's gardens", page 35).

(Coll. M. Sclaresky)

910. - MENTON. - Etude artistique - Vue entre les Oliviers

Hans Georg Tersling (Denmark 1857-Menton 1920), architect on the French Riviera.

The Palais Carnolès and Palais de l'Europe in Menton, as well as Cap Martin, the Villa Masséna in Nice and the Bristol in Beaulieu... Who would have thought that all these buildings could be the work of one architect, Hans Georg Tersling, a Dane who lived in Menton and had his own unique vision of the French Riviera? An architect worthy of greater attention, he is responsible for some of the major works of the 1900s, including many of the French Riviera's elegant palaces and villas.

The good life in Menton.

In Menton, it is also important to take the time to enjoy the seafront itself, with the aptly named "Promenade du Soleil", or to sunbathe on the Sablettes beach just below the old town. Stroll along the old port and past the Palais de l'Europe, once the casino, and then the Palais Carnolès, the Russian church, the church of Saint-Michel, the museum and wedding hall decorated by Jean Cocteau, and the present-day casino. Not to be missed, the Menton lemon festival is held in February-March, at the same time as the orchid show. There are plenty of things to keep you busy during your stay in this adorable little town.

The port in the old town. (Coll. M. Sclaresky)

FRENCH RIVIERA

Albert of Monaco, an ancestor of the current prince.
(Orsay - photo RMN - Hervé Lewandowski)

Monaco: skyscrapers surrounded by blue.

MONACO

The Ligurians, the first sedentary inhabitants of the region, have been described as frugal, hard-working mountain dwellers. From this prehistoric era, we then fast-forward into modern times, since the precise history of Monaco is only really known from the 12th century onwards.

The Grimaldis of Guelfe laid the first stone of the stronghold that stood on the site of today's royal palace. The Emperor, Henry VI, gave sovereignty over all the land surrounding the rock of Monaco to the Grimaldi's chief, Fulco del Castello. In order to attract inhabitants, he offered land concessions and tax exemption to new settlers.

In 1997, the Principality celebrated the 700th anniversary of the Grimaldi

THE MYTH OF THE FRENCH RIVIERA

family's succession in Monaco. For the entire duration of the French Revolution, the Monegasque royal family suffered terrible times, and the wife of Joseph Grimaldi (second son of Honoré III) was guillotined in 1794.

Later on, the Prince was to hand the towns of Menton and Roquebrune over to the French, and the Principality thereby lost 80% of its territory whilst ensuring that its independence was finally recognised. France agreed to build a coastal road linking Nice to Monaco.

During the last century, all forms of direct taxes were abolished. The *Société des Bains de Mer et du Cercle des Etrangers* was entrusted to François Blanc for fifty years and given a monopoly over all gambling activities, and the Principality of Monaco became a constitutional monarchy. In the 1950s, Prince Rainier III married Miss Grace Patricia Kelly, and they had three children, Princess Caroline, Crown Prince Albert and Princess Stephanie. The Principality later lost its beloved Princess Grace in a tragic car accident.

The writer that best captured the sense of cruelty, confinement and grandeur of the very rich, who best described the wealthy but at times icy atmosphere of their luxury hotels and how horribly alone one can feel when surrounded by such enormous wealth, was Edith Wharton. It was she who told the disenchanted tale of what this can bring, and what it can take it away. *"House of Mirth"* is the story of a young woman who, upon her mother's death, refuses to let go of the glittering, ferocious world that no longer wants her in its ranks.

Monaco's most symbolic visitor has to have been Karl Marx in April 1882.

For Scott Fitzgerald, beauty was synonymous with neatness.

Why Monte-Carlo?

The Spélugues plateau is called Monte-Carlo in honour of Prince Charles III.

CAP-D'AIL

The name Cap-d'Ail is thought to come from "Torre d'Abeglio", or the tower of bees that beekeepers built to protect the honey production from hungry wild animals. A contraction of the name Cap d'Abeglio gave rise to the present name of Cap-d'Ail.

Here, in the Villa "Les Funambules" where he was a guest for many years, Sacha Guitry wrote many of his works. Greta Garbo stayed regularly at the villa "The Rock" at Cap Rognosso, and Guillaume Apollinaire, who had studied in Monaco, could often be seen walking along the magnificent "Sentier des Douaniers" coastal footpath.

Beaulieu: saffron and coral alight at sunset.

(The house, standing like the prow of a ship facing the Mediterranean Sea, with its bay window half-hidden by myrtle and lentisk trees, leaves us wondering... Opening the window must be like stepping into the Garden of Eden itself. Who is the lucky occupant? Did this house already exist in Apollinaire's time? Was he a guest there?)

The Lumière brothers owned several villas at Cap-d'Ail, one of which has since been renamed the "Villa Lumière".

Winston Churchill was a regular visitor here, setting up his easel at the Villa Capuncina where he would stay for several months, year after year.

The Prince of Wales, the tsarevitch and many other historic celebrities have also left their mark on Cap d'Ail.

BEAULIEU

This whole section of the coast is caught between sky and sea, winding amongst beautiful villas and impressive rococo palaces ornately decorated in a distinctly "passé" style. Cypress and olive trees, adorable beaches and coves, steep hillsides scattered with lemon, banana and palm trees, as well as mimosa, a blaze of yellow for just a handful of days each winter.

There is a yacht club and sailing club at the port of Beaulieu, home to pretty sun-tanned girls in striped swimsuits, where at times it seems as if the pre-crash period of the "Roaring Twenties" was only yesterday. In the luxury hotels, gold visitors' books keep a record of their illustrious visitors, like at The Métropole, where US presidents, Italian kings, fashion designers, poets, famous journalists, millionaires, dukes and duchesses have all stayed in the style to which they are accustomed, the style of the French Riviera.

"They had dinner at the Palm Beach in Monte-Carlo. Later, much later, near Beaulieu, they disappeared into an open-air grotto outlined by the moonlight, and swam for a long time in between the blue rocks, where the water was phosphorescent, like a basin of mother-or-pearl, with the lights of Monte-Carlo opposite them and, further off, Menton shimmering dimly. She was glad that he

THE MYTH OF THE FRENCH RIVIERA

VILLEFRANCHE

The first thing that strikes you here is the light and the spectacular scenery of this natural amphitheatre that protects the bay from high winds. These are the final summits of the Southern Alps, forming a soft, green setting for this jewel of a village. Villefranche sits by the sea, with its mysterious old town and shady, narrow streets, and the ochre buildings of the citadel with its museums and fragrant gardens. The climate here has enchanted royalty and stars alike, and the setting attracts many filmmakers desperate to use it as the perfect backdrop. Villefranche-sur-Mer is intimate, friendly and peaceful, an extraordinary

A handful of pretty little houses by the sea at Villefranche.

A little, pocket-sized harbour.

had brought her there, to the eastern end of the Riviera, to give her a new view of the wind on the water. As new as they were to each other, she was lying across the saddle, like a symbol of abduction, as if he had captured her in Damascus and they were galloping confidently across the Mongolian plains. Everything that Dick had taught her fell away from her little by little, and she came to resemble more and more the person she was before him [...]

They woke together. The moon had gone. The air was cooler. She asked him what time it was. About three, he thought.

"I have to go."

"I thought we could go and sleep in Monte-Carlo"

Tender is the Night, F.S. Fitzgerald

little town that seems to tumble down the hillside and stop just at the water's edge. It has been home to poets of every possible style and language, whose presence has contributed to making this town a veritable Mecca for poetry-lovers.

(Coll. M. Sclaresky)

"And that night, in front of my open window, like a picture frame around the ongoing discussion between the lighthouse and the red light on the breakwater, the sharp light of the clear moon over the still water, and the boats floating in emptiness...".

This pretty little town will forever be linked to Cocteau, who loved and lived there and drew comfort from the place, in as much as he could, since by his own admission he never really got over the death of Radiguet, that prodigal son, the young, scandalous author of *"Diable au Corps"*.

Another excellent writer of those times to fall in love with Villefranche and with the Riviera in general was Morand, a man always in a hurry and whose brilliance would eventually harm his writing.

Cocteau lived for a long time at the Welcome Hotel on the port - "a dispensary of dreams" which still stands today. Prices are reasonable, although the hotel is no doubt more impersonal than it was at the time. The Cocteau effect is a little overdone but this is nevertheless a perfect spot, especially off-season. Morand on the other hand chose to buy the Orangerie at the Corne d'Or, and Blaise Cendrars also bought a house here. Evelyn Waugh, a disagreeable person if ever there was one, but a most enjoyable writer, used to say that all the bores came to the Riviera, yet he also lived at the Welcome Hotel and would dine every other night at the Connollys, or at Aldous Huxley's or at Maugham's!

SAINT-JEAN-CAP-FERRAT

It is the western part of this sublime peninsula that has given Cap-Ferrat its 'multimillionaire' reputation.

After his years at the 'hotel-brothel' in Villefranche, Jean Cocteau came to live here, from 1950 onwards, at the Villa Santo-Sospir, the home of Francine Weisweiller. Incapable of staying there without anything to do, he decided to paint the walls and then the floors and ceilings with such cherished themes of his as Greek mythology, the Mediterranean, and the pine trees of Nice. In 1926, Somerset Maugham also decided to settle in Saint-Jean-Cap-Ferrat, buying the Villa La Mauresque, which had been built in

The chapel in Villefranche decorated by Cocteau. Jade and turquoise like the waters of the Riviera.

1806 for King Leopold II of Belgium, where he used to entertain his neighbour, Jean Cocteau.

Lauren Bacall, Romy Schneider, and Gregory Peck also lived in Saint-Jean-Cap-Ferrat. The Marnier-Lapostole family's villa has one of the French Riviera's most beautiful exotic gardens, where a large collection of plant essences, used in the making of Grand Marnier, is to be found.

Half hidden by the surrounding greenery...

... some beautiful houses by the sea.

Nice: the port.

Place Massena.

NICE

Today, Nice is a thriving centre for art and culture. The city is built around the Place Masséna, its geographical centre, built from 1832 onwards after several successive projects. In 1852, Nice named the square Masséna in honour of one of the city's illustrious citizens. Nice and its coastline have inspired painters, writers and musicians. Painters like Chagall, Matisse, Toulouse-Lautrec, Modigliani, Dufy, Renoir, Picasso, writers such as Prévert, Nietzsche, Aragon, Tolstoy, and Maupassant, and musicians such as Berlioz, Bizet and Massenet were all truly fascinated by this city, not to mention the many architects that have left their mark on the city. Nice is unique, unlike any other provincial city. The

THE MYTH OF THE FRENCH RIVIERA

The Promenade des Anglais (Coll. M. Sclaresky)

cultural, aesthetic atmosphere that reigns there is kept alive today by artists like Le Clézio, Yves Klein, Ben, Malaval, Viallat and César, and the city seems to be in a perpetual fever of excitement.

"For the inhabitants of Nice, any traveller is English. Each foreigner, without distinction of hair, beard, clothing, age and gender, comes from the same fantastical city lost in the fog, where occasionally there is some vague talk of sunshine, where oranges and pineapples are known by name alone, and where the only ripe fruits are stewed apples; that city must be called London.

Whilst I was staying at the Hôtel d'York, a carriage arrived, and a moment later, the innkeeper entered my room.

One of the legendary luxury hotels.

Occitan

Occitan is the name given to a set of dialects that stem from the old, medieval "langue d'oc". The Niçois language, or "nissart", is one of these dialects. With similarities to Provençal and to langue d'oc itself, it has remained very much a Romance language. Nice's turbulent history has of course left its mark on the city's dialect, which has incorporated Ligurian, Roman, Provençal, Piedmont, Italian and lastly French vocabulary, without losing its identity. The local population pronounces the dialect in their own unique way, and it was the only language spoken here until the early 20th century. Nissart is taught at university level where it given the same importance as other Latin languages.

"What are your newcomers?" I asked him.

"Sono certi Inglesi", he answered, "manon saprei dire se sono Francesi o Tedeschi".

Which means: They are certainly English, but I could not say whether they are French or German.

(Alexandre Dumas, "Impressions de Voyage").

The old town of Nice with added colour.
(Coll. M. Sclaresky)

221. - NICE. - Vue générale prise du Mont Boron - Entrée du Port

The Palais Maeterlinck, Palais Orlamonde

The Palais Maeterlinck with its fascinating history is one of the most beautiful, astonishing, bizarre and splendid palaces on the French Riviera.

It is a timeless place, former residence of the count and poet, Maurice Maeterlinck, and formerly an ostentatious casino launched by a Russian aristocrat in 1920. Work ceased in 1928 due to lack of funds and the building has never been finished.

This little corner of paradise in its grandiose setting overlooking the sea, became the Villa Orlamonde, "the meeting place for high society on the Riviera". In the lounge and atrium, with its fountains and colonnades, the poet would play host to the likes of Martin du Gard, André Gide and Jules Romains.

The old town of Nice needs no added colour.

Orlamonde became a legendary place, and was the setting for Maeterlinck's boyhood memoirs entitled "Bulles bleues, souvenirs heureux".

Speaking of him, Antonin Artaud said, "Maeterlinck has the gift of splendid language. It is impossible to analyse his thoughts. His philosophy is right there in this gift that he has of using images to reveal obscure sensations and unknown lines of thought."

Orlamonde was looted several times during the Second World War when Maeterlinck was in the United States.

Following Maurice Maeterlinck's death, and later that of his wife Renée, the Villa Orlamonde was abandoned for many years until it became nothing but a shadow of its former self. Then in the 1980s, a Swiss businessman fell under the spell of this sleeping beauty and began to restore the villa.

Today the Hotel-Palais Maeterlinck, located on the lower coastal road at the Cap de Nice between the Port of Nice and the Bay of Villefranche, sits in 3.5 hectares of cypress trees, olive trees and lavender, perched on the cliff tops overlooking the Mediterranean Sea.

All rooms and apartments have one or more terraces with a sea view, and the only sound to be heard is the breaking of the waves on the rocks below.

25

One can spend hours watching the yachts in the port of Antibes.

The market in Antibes.

ANTIBES

Antibes, the most Greek of all French towns, was founded by Greek sailors, most likely Phœnicians, in the 5th-6th centuries BC (the date is rather uncertain). The town - *polis* - was christened Antipolis, meaning "the town opposite"...but opposite what? Since it was used as a marker for Greek sailors arriving from Corsica, the "town opposite" was therefore Antibes.

Far from the high society of Cannes and Monte-Carlo, life in Antibes is peaceful, slow and cosseted. The town is surrounded by sea and mountains and has attracted its fair share of admirers.

André Breton looking everywhere for the laughing, unfaithful Suzanne in "Nadja", who ran off with Emmanuel Berl one day during carnival.

Gérard de Nerval also came here to forget his disappointed love for Jenny Colon.

Graham Greene took an apartment with a view of the port, wrote a great deal and thought little of love.

Ernst Jünger mentions the Rue de Sade in *"Contemplateur solitaire"*: "Amongst its narrow streets I have to mention the Rue de Sade, because of its name. There is not yet enough indifference to morality for the street to be thus named in honour of the divine Marquis. Rather, for centuries, the street has been named after his powerful family, who originally came from this area. Nevertheless, each time I pass by there and glance at the street sign, I feel a little shiver of scandal from "One hundred and twenty days of Sodom".

"The jujube factory
an old street in Antibes
four thousand inhabitants. Panoramic view
gentle steps for asthmatics
The Fort Vauban shaped like a boat; the thirteenth century church; the tower could be made of wax. Nets are mended under the plane trees,
and the shade is like cooling water on the children's brows. Despite its ramparts
and all the ancient war apparel,
the officers and soldiers,
as if softened by such a mild climate,
do not have a military air to them at all.
But then again, I know nothing of these things."

Max Jacob

THE CAP D'ANTIBES

"The little town, closed in behind heavy military walls built by Mr. de Vauban, stretches into the sea in the middle of the vast Bay of Nice. The high waves roll in and break at its feet, surrounding it with flowers of foam. And above the ramparts, houses climb one on top of each other up to two towers, standing in the sky like two horns on an ancient helmet. And these two towers are outlined against the milky whiteness of the Alps, a huge and distant wall of snow across the entire horizon. Between the white foam beneath the city walls and the white snow on the horizon, the little town stands shining against the bluish background of the mountains, offering up to the rays of the setting sun a pyramid of red roofed houses; their walls are white too, and yet so different that there seems to be many different shades. And the sky above the Alps is also nearly white, as if bleached by the snow, and a few silvery clouds float near the pale summits. And on the other side of the bay, Nice stands by the sea, stretching out like a white thread between the sea and mountains. Two large lateen sails, pushed forward by a strong breeze, seem to skip across the waves."
(Guy de Maupassant, "Madame Parisse").

It was Vauban who ordered the construction of Antibes' ramparts.

The Cap d'Antibes is home to one of the oldest shipwrecks on the Provençal coast...an Etruscan ship which sank around 525 BC, long before the trading post of Antipolis was founded.

JUAN-LES-PINS

It is the summer of 1926, an outstanding season, the epitome of a perfect summer. The dollar is worth thirty-six francs. The Fitzgeralds are about to face two major turning points: the first, the writer's thirtieth birthday, seems unavoidable, but as yet, the couple is unaware of the second event, as are all the Americans holidaying on the Riviera (the well-to-do French and British winter visitors to the Riviera would not be seen dead here in summer), and that is the stock market crash of October 1929.

The Fitzgeralds have rented the Villa Paquita and then, thanks to the sale of the copyright to "Gatsby", the Villa Saint-Louis, which today is the Hotel Belles Rives. Fitzgerald writes to a friend: "There is nobody here except Zelda and me, the Valentinos, Mistinguett, Dos Passos, Etienne de Beaumont, E. Philip Oppenheim, Marguerite Namara, the former Prime Minister Orlando, Mannes the cellist..." Truly, nobody at all! And he had forgotten Hemingway, Anita Loos (Gentlemen prefer blondes), Rebecca West...

In that same summer of 1926, Maurice Sachs writes of the Juan-Les-Pins of Picasso, Marie Laurencin, the Countess of Chambrun... Love stories run their course, causing scandals, heartbreak and gossip, laughter and tears.... It is the summer of 1926 in Juan-Les-Pins...

"The hotel had a golden beach that stretched below it like a prayer mat. In the early morning light, the distant image of Cannes, the pink and cream colour of the old ramparts, the reflection of the purple-shaded Alps, barring the way to Italy, shimmered in the bay, shifting as the waves broke on the seaweed along the seashore."
(F.S. Fitzgerald)

Happy times for Scott and Zelda Fitzgerald.

The Hotel Belles Rives, formerly the Villa Saint-Louis, deserves to be famous. It is a timeless corner of paradise in an enchanting setting, steeped in history, a place with a soul.
The Fitzgeralds spent their best season there, before things began their downward spiral. It was a summer of wealth and glory, youth and love.
The sepia coloured photos of that time show the young Zelda with lovely bare arms and a fresh little face, sitting under the climbing roses on the stone steps of the villa.
There are women like Zelda who leave their own magical touch in certain places, and later Marianne Estène-Chauvin was to do the same.

Hotel Belles-Rives.

Cannes...

CANNES

Little can be said about Cannes that has not already been said, written or heard. How to break away from the town's image as a focal point for the stars, a superb city that is the stage for so many festivals and the backdrop to the most unforgettable parties?

Glitter and stars shine mainly at night.

Irresistible red and blue in Saint-Tropez.

SAINT-TROPEZ

"[...] on the abandoned beach, seashells and shellfish... I'll take the train back to the autumn, to a rainy city, I'll share my grief with nobody, I'll keep it as a friend... The Mistral will get used to blowing on empty seas, and it is in my tousled hair that I'll miss it the most."

Without further ado, let us shed a tear for the Saint-Tropez that used to be. The Saint-Tropez of (in no particular order) BB and Colette, the first topless sunbathers and scandalous swimsuits, pretty girls in leather sandals, superb 1950s wooden yachts, beach parties with no sponsors... Or the earlier "Saint-Trop" of Maupassant on his yacht "Bel Ami" ("a nice little town, salty and courageous"), when the only link between the village and the outside world was a small steam train and an old stagecoach.

Once and for all, let's acknowledge that "no longer in Saint Tropez do you go from pleasure to pleasure, from secret rendezvous to secret rendezvous, from one corner of the beach to another. From one room to another, from dinner with X to dinner with Y, from club no.1 to club no. 2, or at night from one crowd to another, and by day from one boutique to another. You no longer live like a happy hunter or consenting prey; you go from clan to clan and story to story. Like in a Greek tragedy, but by a vaudeville Euripides inspired by Feydeau the sociologist, love only exists if it is commented upon, beaches only if you pay for the mattresses, and desire only if it is marketable." (Françoise Sagan *"Avec mon meilleur souvenir"*)

There was a time here when you would run into Sartre sitting at a table outside the Sénéquier, or at the Flore or elsewhere. So what? So you see Sartre at the Sénéquier, what are you going to do? Ask for an autograph, or take a photo, hoping he will kiss the girl sitting next to him?

So, the truth is out. Saint-Tropez is not what it used to be. Who or what is to blame? Times changing, the introduction of paid holiday leave and the democratisation of summer holidays? And would things be any better if the town had just become some sort of ghetto for rich people?

Let's say it again. Saint-Tropez is not what it used to be. In *"Douceur de veillir"*, Maurice Goudeket writes of a Saint-Tropez unspoiled by tourists, a nonchalant little port, with painted houses, the sailor's ball, time passing, blue by night and golden by day...

[...] It was paradise, with plenty of deserted beaches backed by pine forests. A Tahitian lifestyle, entire days spent in swimming costumes, cooking under the trees right next to the beach. Clear waters by day, lively cafés by night, music and dancing all along the port. In the morning, having breakfast in a café, I could see all the yachts being cleaned and polished for the day ahead. A beautiful, lively place. Heat, lethargy, thirst, long cycle rides. Flowering and softness, brightly coloured beachwear. Girls sitting topless on convertibles, the pleasure was intense, as if we all knew that this would be the last fine summer..."

(Diaries of Anaïs Nin)

But you can find this Saint-Trop' again, in May, in September, or in winter, any time you don't go there with the August crowds to pay an extortionate price for a glass of rosé. All you have to do is look for it, whether you are rich or not, whether you hide at a friend's house up in the hills or you just go for a hamburger and some excellent French fries at the Gorille.

It's like everything else. You just have to go there at the right time. And if you have to go in August, unless you go at four in the morning when dawn is breaking and the evening's revellers are going home to bed, then try to tread lightly!

Saint-Tropez' seductive charm is revealed at dusk.

31

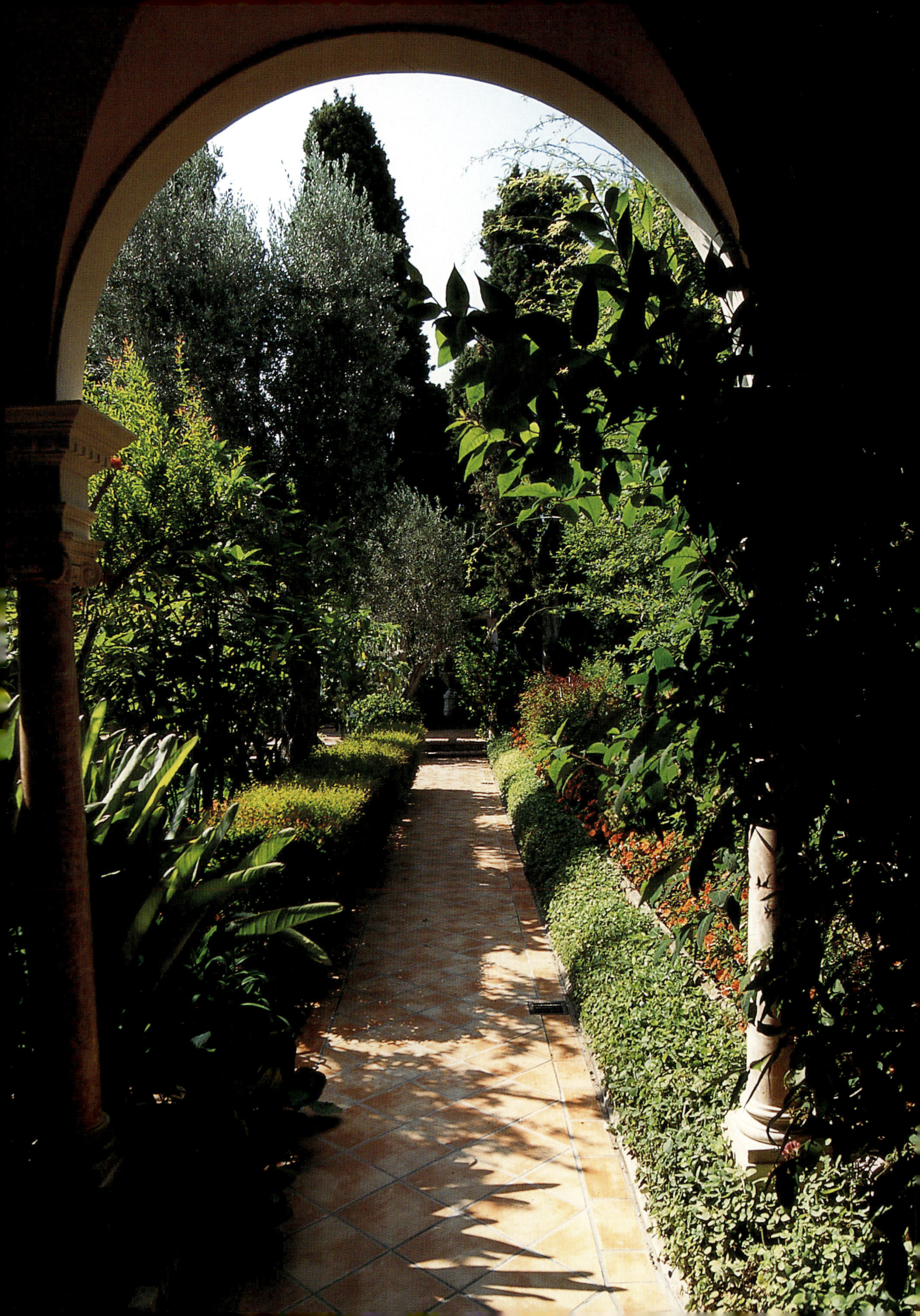

Discovering the Riveria's gardens

**Menton
Sainte-Agnès
Monaco
Eze
Beaulieu-sur-Mer
Saint-Jean-Cap-Ferrat
Nice
Cagnes-sur-Mer
Biot
Mougins
Cap d'Antibes
Juan-les-Pins
Ile Sainte-Marguerite
Les jardins du Rayol**

"Spring had crossed my path, spring as you imagine it in a fairy tale, the exuberant, ephemeral, irresistible spring of the South of France, fat, fresh, bursting forth in a riot of greenery, in grass already long and blowing and shimmering in the wind, in mauve Judas trees, in grey periwinkle coloured paulownias, in laburnums, in wisteria, in roses..." (Colette)

The French Riviera's climate, one imagines, is much like the climate in paradise. As a result, this extraordinary region is home to a generous array of plants: brightly coloured hibiscus and bougainvillaea, plenty of jasmine and honeysuckle, small, sharp little roses in spring and cauliflower roses in the autumn that shed their petals in winter, palm and cypress trees, citrus trees and hundred-year-old olive trees, rich in fruit and full of character, growing in the countryside and on the terraced hillsides overlooking the sea.

The gardens of the French Riviera are elegant, sensual, sometimes secret and often daring... In fact, they represent a whole art of life.

Balancing shade and sun according to the seasons, planting hedges against the north winds, managing water, the life blood of any garden... here, these are practices as old as the earth itself. Small village squares are shaded by large trees - plane trees, lime trees and southern nettle trees. Inside the old Provençal farmhouses there are sheltered corners for taking tea or eating outdoors under a gazebo laced with wisteria, Virginia creeper and passionflower. Often there are several of these corners, one for each time of the day or year.

The French Riviera has its own unique garden heritage. As elsewhere in Provence, until the end of the 18th century, the art of life was at once Roman and Romanesque. Then, an English, Russian and American elite created the "Riviera" along with the first of the French artists, writers, painters and even diplomats to come South to enjoy this subtropical climate. Many of them had the means to indulge their most extraordinary whims in the field of landscape gardening, in the choice of architecture and of unforgettable places in which to stop a while (the Riviera is full of such spots). But it was the English who introduced a vast range of exotic species which today have become an integral part of the landscape, such as palm trees, agave, banana trees, eucalyptus, hibiscus, prickly pear, aloe...

A magical archway in the Ephrussi de Rothschild gardens.

Biot.

FRENCH RIVIERA

With the arrival of this new form of tourist, Cannes evolved from a simple fishing village to the sophisticated town that we know today, and Monaco opened a casino next to its railway station.

All along this beautiful stretch of coast that is the Riviera are some of the most beautiful gardens in existence, a delight to the eyes, nose and in fact, to all the senses. Some of the most remarkable are the Rayol gardens, and the appropriately named Serres de la Madone (*the Madonna's greenhouse*) gardens in Menton.

The Rayol gardens are breathtaking, in a luxurious setting of coves, pine trees and cicada, tiny heavenly beaches surrounded by ancient trees and alive with the scent of resin. The Serres de la Madone gardens are one of the most romantic settings on the Riviera, like a fairy tale... Indeed, if fairies do exist then they must surely live here, brushing past the moss covered nose of a statue, somersaulting over

DISCOVERING THE RIVIERA'S GARDENS

the water in the ponds and playing leapfrog with the dragonflies.

Together, all these legendary gardens form a unique heritage. Many have been restored and are open to the public, in particular in Menton, or at La Mortola, just over the border in Italy, and at Cap-Ferrat, where Beatrice de Rothschild let her imagination run wild, inspired by her many journeys all over the world.

THE MEDIEVAL GARDEN OF SAINTE-AGNÈS
Sainte-Agnès

This charming garden at the top of the village of Sainte-Agnès is definitely worth a visit. It is an ideal place for a walk in the fresh air, combining beautiful scenery and views with an extraordinary work of meticulous patience. The Mediterranean plants and familiar trees on display here look much like embroidery, a jigsaw puzzle of wooded areas and maquis.

Open all year round.

THE VAL RAHMEH BOTANICAL GARDENS
Avenue Saint-Jacques, 06500 Menton

Lord Radcliffe created these gardens at the end of the 19th century on land that used to belong to peasant farmers. The olive grove from this time remains today (the Pian olive grove). In 1966, Miss Campbell, a rich and eccentric

The honey sweet smell of broom in the spring air.

The path to the gardens at Sainte-Agnès.

FRENCH RIVIERA

Englishwoman and botany enthusiast, sold the land to the Museum of Natural History. Sheltered from the cold north winds, nestling in the hollow of a circle of mountains, hot and humid and protected from frost, Val Rahmeh is the ideal location for the introduction and acclimatisation of tropical plants. A large fountain and ornamental lake by the English landscape gardener Humphrey Waterfield is home to the famous Indian lotus that flowers in late June, early July. It houses a range of subtropical species as well as a rare outdoor example of *Sophora Toromiro*. The gardens have now become the Mediterranean branch of the French Museum of Natural History.

Open all year round. Admission charge.

FONTANA ROSA GARDENS - JARDIN DES ROMANCIERS
Avenue Blasco-Ibanez,
06500 Menton

Listed as an historic monument, this garden, which Vincent Blasco Ibanez bought in 1921, is located on the outskirts of Menton, in the Bay of Garavan. The site resembles a kind of open-air reading room with benches and earthenware fountains surrounded by Mediterranean plants and a wealth of subtropical species.

Open Fridays at 10 a.m. Guided tours only.

GARDENS OF THE VILLA MARIA SERENA
21, promenade Reine-Astrid,
06500 Menton

These gardens were designed by Charles Garnier, architect of the Paris Opera House, for his friend Ferdinand de Lesseps. The park mainly comprises tropical and subtropical species, palm trees, cycads and bird of paradise.

Open Tuesdays from 10 a.m., all year round. Guided tour.

THE "SERRE DE LA MADONE" GARDENS
74, route de Gorbio, 06500 Menton

Listed as an historic monument, this is a little corner of paradise on earth, rather like a love story with a happy end. It is the work of

Above: **The ochre facade of the villa in the Val Rameh gardens.**

The "Serre de la Madone" gardens, the most romantic on the Riviera.

Laurence Johnston, who also designed the famous Hidcote Manor gardens in England. He built this garden on the slopes of the Gorbio valley between 1919 and 1939. Having travelled around the world and in particular in Asia, Major Johnston brought back a rich botanical collection and transformed a simple hillside into an extraordinary garden, achieving surprisingly successful acclimatisation thanks to Menton's mild climate. Terraces, rock gardens, pergolas, water mirrors and orange groves lost in a sea of plants, bursting with colours and scents... The gardens seem almost wild, and yet the wildness is a deliberate attempt to create the feeling of being the first visitor on a deserted island. Everything here is clearly designed to allow each visitor to discover their own personal paradise. There are no straight and unsurprising paths leading arrogantly towards a place that the visitor has already seen in advan-

FRENCH RIVIERA

trees and the impressive development of around forty species that to this day have no known equivalent elsewhere. Over and above their botanical importance, these gardens are a remarkable work of landscape gardening. They are currently being restored and are protected by the National Coastal Conservancy.

Guided tours every Friday at 2.30 pm (contact the Heritage Department of the City of Menton). Admission charge.

JAPANESE GARDEN
Avenue Princesse-Grace, MC 98000 Monaco

Here in 70 000 square metres on the very edge of the Mediterranean, lies the most classical Japanese garden in

The "Serre de la Madone" gardens with the house of their designer, Laurence Johnston.

Right: **Every little detail of the "Serre de la Madone" is magical.**

ce. Here, desire and pleasure are the first priority, and if you just follow your nose and not a marked itinerary, you may well find yourself under a gazebo of flowers. From a botanical point of view, the greenhouses are fascinating. An inventory of botanical species has revealed some rare

Europe. Surrounded by the sea and crowned by stars, the garden was blessed by a Shintoist grand priest and is all that one might expect of a Japanese garden: stone, water, grass and plants all cohabit in perfect harmony under a set of strictly observed rules.

A rose is a rose.

Open all year round, from 9 a.m. to sunset.

In early summer, cosmos sway slowly in the sea breeze in the "Serre de la Madone" gardens.

THE FONTVIEILLE LANDSCAPED GARDENS AND THE PRINCESS GRACE ROSE GARDEN
Fontvieille, MC 98000 Monaco

Five thousand five hundred rose bushes, including two hundred and forty rare species, planted in memory of Princess Grace who loved them so much.

Open all year round, from sunrise to sunset.

JARDIN EXOTIQUE DE MONACO
62, boulevard du Jardin-Exotique, BP 105 MC 98002 Monaco

Augustin Gastaud, a municipal gardener in Monaco, once designed a small cactus garden on the Rock of Monaco out of his love for the strange shapes of these succulent plants. Prince Albert, a great oceanographer and founder of the Oceanographic Museum, fascinated by these curious plants, asked the chief engineer of the Principality of Monaco to find a sheltered spot to develop these plants. Thus, at the end of the last century, the Jardin Exotique was begun in Monaco and opened to the public in 1933.

The "Jardin Exotique de Monaco" with its collection of elegant, spiky cacti.

A visit to the gardens is a journey to more exotic climes, with 6000 varieties of semi-desert flora. At the bottom of the garden, visit the even more exotic cave, the *"Grotte de l'Observatoire"*, which adds the finishing touches to this exceptional site. There is a magnificent view of the Rock of Monaco, the port, Monte-Carlo, Fontvieille, Cap-Martin and the Italian Riviera.

Open all year round (except November 19 and December 25). Admission charge.

EXOTIC GARDENS OF EZE
20, rue du Château, 06360 Eze

This rocky landscaped garden perched above some of the most exceptional scenery always offers a panoramic view of sky and sea. The gardens stand next to a sheer drop over the Mediterranean and are built on the site of the ruined medieval castle of Eze overlooking the village. Here the Gastaud family of French horticulturist (responsible for planting at the Jardin Exotique de Monaco) has developed an important collection of succulent plants.

Open daily all year round. Admission charge.

FRENCH RIVIERA

The Villa Kerylos overlooking the Baie des Fourmis.
(Photos Institut de France – Fondation Théodore Reinach)

KERYLOS VILLA AND GARDENS
Fondation Théodore Reinach, rue Gustave-Eiffel, 06310 Beaulieu-sur-Mer

This garden with its Mediterranean trees sits by the sea overlooking the Baie des Fourmis, offering some of the most magnificent views from Cap-Ferrat to Monaco. This garden by the sea comprises an interpretation path, explaining the symbolism of the plants along the way. As for the Villa Kerylos, built on this coastal promontory at the Pointe des Fourmis, it is one of a kind, a reconstitution of the sumptuous décor of an ancient Greek villa. Fine and precious materials were used for the furniture, frescos and mosaics that are all exact reproductions based on ancient Greek illustrations.

The Villa Kerylos was built between 1902 to 1908 at the request of Theodore Reinach (1860 – 1928), a musicographer, archaeologist, numismatist, member of the Institut de France and Member of Parliament for Savoy. The villa is the work of the architect Emmanuel Pontremoli, his colleague from the Academy of Fine Arts and winner of the Grand Prix de Rome in 1890. Kerylos, which means halcyon (a sea bird and good omen), is breathtakingly beautiful. Not even in Greece can one find such a fine example of how the ancient Greeks used to live and what their houses contained in the time of Pericles. Nothing has been left out, and all traces of modern comfort are cunningly concealed: mirrors, electricity, the piano...

Founded: 1902. Open all year round except from November 11 to mid-December, December 25 and January 1st. Admission charge.

The classical beauty of the Villa Kerylos.
(Photo Institut de France – Fondation Théodore Reinach).

There is something particularly charming about the gardens surrounding the Villa Kerylos.
(Photo Institut de France – Fondation Théodore Reinach).

Even if the Villa Ephrussi de Rothschild has something a little too spruce, a little too sweet about it...

GARDENS AND VILLA EPHRUSSI DE ROTHSCHILD
Avenue Denis-Semeria,
06230 Saint-Jean-Cap-Ferrat

An exceptional estate in an exceptional location, at the highest point of the Saint-Jean-Cap-Ferrat peninsula, with views eastwards over the Baie des Fourmis and the Italian Riviera, and westwards towards the Bay of Villefranche and the Esterel mountains. The villa, now a museum, is a Venetian inspired *palazzino* housing a rich collection of paintings, furniture, porcelain, tapestries and sculptures. The villa is surrounded by seven theme gardens (Spanish, Florentine, Japanese, Provençal, Oriental, exotic and French), through which you can stroll as if on the decks of an ocean liner.

Academy of Fine Arts of the *Institut de France*.

The garden is listed as an historic monument.

Open all year round. Admission charge.

... its gardens are nevertheless among the most beautiful on the French Riviera.

45

THE FINEST GARDENS IN NICE

Jardin du Monastère
The Jardin du Monastère is an ideal spot for all those who enjoy peace and quiet and open views. The old pergolas leaning against the monastery are covered with perpetually flowering climbing roses. Orange, bitter orange and mandarin trees stand amidst a very well kept lawn and nearby, the "holy" wood encourages meditation.

Jardin Albert I
One of the oldest gardens in Nice and the first to link the old town to the new town. Located in the city centre next to the sea, it stretches up to the Esplanade du Paillon, the Square Leclerc and the Promenade du Paillon, forming a green line of gardens stretching for a whole 2-km inland from the beach.

Parc Pheonix
This park boasts the largest greenhouse in Europe, an astronomical garden, an Island of Past Times, exotic fish, birds and butterflies, thousands of flowers and many exhibitions and events. It is a place for discovery and new experiences. More than 2500 species of plants are on display in these vast botanical gardens, organised around ten themes, each with different environments: aquatic, desert, Mediterranean, tropical etc, and covering a range of different aspects: discovery, flora, ecology, ethno-botany etc. The lake and enormous aviary are home to more than 70 species of birds. The huge tropical greenhouse, over 7000 square metres, contains seven different climate zones: the central tropical zone and carnivorous plants, the orchid-bromeliads, the southern zone (South Africa), the fern zone, the Louisiana zone (houseplants), the butterfly house and the exhibition zone. As well as this exceptional botanical collection, the greenhouse also contains seawater and freshwater aquariums, and an insectarium with spiders and turtles.
Open daily. Admission charge.

On the pond's smooth surface, the overhanging leaves cast dark shadows on the water. A dragonfly skims over the pond, drinks and flies off again.

The botanical gardens of Nice
These are distinctly Mediterranean gardens, first planted in May 1983 using a collection of 100 species owned by the Natural History Museum. The gardens were opened to the public in 1991 and make for an interesting stroll through a collection of plants and typical landscapes. The park's design is closely linked to the rhythm of the plants themselves, all of which are grown from seed, and one zone is reserved for growing endangered species.

The Parc du Château
Here lies the Nice's birthplace, steeped in history and legends, of which the only remains are the ruins of the cathedral of Notre-Dame-du-Château. The park is peaceful, with refreshing waterfalls and remarkable plants. It is also a children's paradise with its varied children's playground, and offers some of the most beautiful views of the Baie des Anges, the old town and the port of Nice.

Parc des Arènes de Cimiez
Situated on the hill of Cimiez, next to the Jardin du Monastère, the Parc des Arènes is the ideal place to spend the day. You can picnic under the olive trees, play on the lawn (no "Keep Off" signs here!) and visit the Archaeology museum, the Matisse museum and the Roman remains of Cemenelum.

Everything here is larger than life, from the showers of bougainvillea to César's thumb.

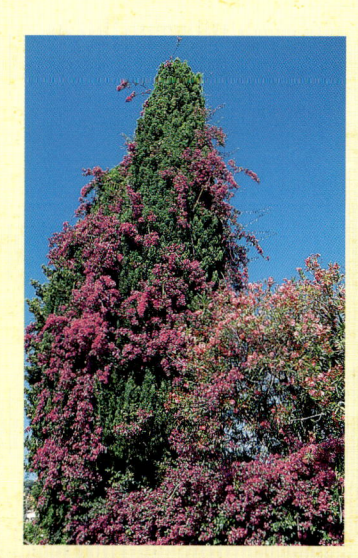

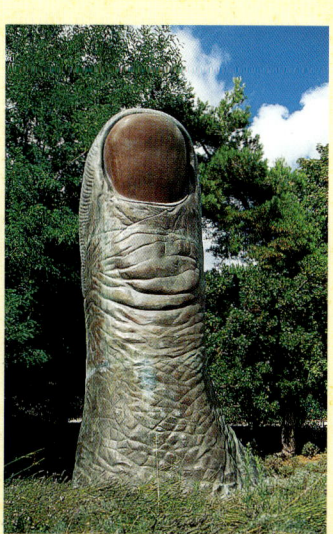

THE AUGUSTE-RENOIR MUSEUM AND GARDENS
Montée des Collettes, 06800 Cagnes-sur-Mer

This was the estate of the French painter Auguste Renoir, where he built a house and studio (now the museum) and where he spent the last years of his life. The original layout has been faithfully preserved, along with many personal and family objects. A dozen of Renoir's paintings are on exhibition. The gardens are very pleasant, with Renoir's huge bronze Venus, "Venus Victrix", on one of the terraces, and rose bushes, orange and lemon trees on another. The garden was founded in 1908 and the olive trees are a century old.

Open daily except Tuesdays. Closed from October 15 to November 15.

Admission charge.

Moss, stone and water: the three essential elements in a Japanese garden.
(photo Gil Lanzi – Bonzaï arboretum).

BONZAI ARBORETUM
299, chemin du Val de Pôme, 06410 Biot

The French Riviera's Bonsai Arboretum is a museum of living sculptures set in a 3000 square metre Japanese garden, with an impressive collection of bonsais from around the world and some quite exceptional trees. Surface area: 4000 square metres. Owner: the Okonek family. Created: 1980.

Open daily except Tuesdays. Open all year round. Admission charge.

ETANG DE FONTMERLE-MOUGINS
Chemin de l'Etang, domaine de Fontmerle, 06250 Mougins

Located in a tourist park at the edge of the Valmasque Regional Park, the aquatic environment of this pond is unique in Europe, thanks to the continuing presence of the perfectly acclimatised lotus (*Nelumbo nucifera*). This plant blooms spectacularly from late June to September. The pond has been restored, by clearing the reed grasses from the bottom to create a balance of reeds, lotus and free stretches of water for birds (ducks, herons, black swans, etc.). The pond is surrounded by typical maquis and garrigue vegetation growing on fresh, damp soil (privet, *nerprum, Lonicera xylostreum*, Pyracantha, blackthorn, red elm, willow and narrowleaf ash) and a remarkable alignment of taxodium (common bald cypress and marsh cypress), conifers rarely found on the French Riviera due to the lack of humidity. These trees stand beautifully tall and turn an attractive reddish-purple colour in autumn. Part of their roots grow above the soil to allow the tree to breathe.

BOTANICAL GARDENS OF THE VILLA THURET
62, boulevard du Cap, 06606 Cap-d'Antibes

The "inventor" of the Villa Thuret was a diplomat before turning to the study of algae at a very young age. In 1857, Gustave Thuret discovered the Cap d'Antibes, a wild spot of surprising beauty. He bought 5 hectares of land on which he built a villa and laboratory, then began to create a fabulous park. He planted a superb collection of exotic plants and shrubs and the next year began testing the acclimatisation of a large range of plants.

Today, this is a scientific botanical garden, specialising in the acclimatisation of plants and shrubs from Mediterranean climates around the world. The site has remained practically as it was when it was founded over a hundred years ago as one of the first acclimatisation gardens on the Riviera. Gustave Thuret died in 1875, and his heirs donated the estate to the nation. The first director was the French botanist, Charles Naudin, who continued to study the acclimatisation to the Mediterranean climate of woody plants from hot regions. In 1927, the property was bought by the National Institute of Agronomic Research as a centre for botany and plant biology.

The scientific botanical gardens at the Villa Thuret.

FRENCH RIVIERA

The luscious island of Sainte-Marguerite.

Open daily except Saturdays, Sundays and holidays. Closed between Christmas and New Year. Free admission.

PARC EXFLORA
RN 7, avenue de Cannes, 06160 Juan-les-Pins

This 5-hectare public park, designed by the landscape gardener, Alain Goudot, was built in the 1990s and takes the visitor on a journey through time and through different civilisations, from ancient Rome to the exuberant Riviera of the 19th century, thanks to a range of dreamlike gardens from around the Mediterranean rim. The entire park can be seen from the Grebel viewpoint, a terrace designed in true Italian Renaissance style. The use of water is particularly fascinating: moss-covered fountains, waterfalls, oases, and a line of ornamental lakes and fountains built in alignment with the belvedere and forming a 500 metre long "path of water". Exotic garden; palm grove; open air theatre (inspired by Italian gardens); a maze of trimmed shrubs inspired by traditional Provençal gardens of the 18th century; the Islamic garden with its criss-cross of terracotta irrigation channels (similar to the famous courtyard of Seville cathedral); the "arsal", the technique of incised cultivation used in Moroccan gardens (a reference to the Riad, or square courtyard found in the centre of Moroccan houses); a pavilion in honour of the painter, Majorelle *(Le Jardin bleu du Marrakech);* and the atrium, peristyle and Pompeii gardens of ancient Rome.

All this and more in this extraordinary location overlooking the Mediterranean and the Iles de Lérins.

ILE SAINTE-MARGUERITE
Iles de Lérins, 06400 Cannes

A walk around this wooded island is quite literally enchanting. It is covered with typical Mediterranean coastal vegetation: eucalyptus, pine trees, arbutus, lentisk, rockrose, rosemary and Estrella gold *(erica arborea)*. Broad avenues lead from one side of the island to another, and the whole island can be visited in just 2 hours. In summer, relax in inviting coves and doze off to the song of cicadas. There is a spectacular view from the Cap Roux to the Cap d'Antibes and of the Ile Saint-Honorat. Surface area: 1,400,000 square metres (14 hectares).

Owned by the French state and managed by the Forestry Commission.

Open to visitors all year round. Accessible by boat from Cannes.

The Rayol Gardens

Until the turn of the century, the coastal part of the Maures mountain range was practically uninhabited, mainly due to difficult access. There were just a few fortified villages along the coastline, such as Saint-Tropez, Ramatuelle and Gassin. With the arrival of the Provence railway line in 1885, the coast at last became accessible and began to open up to tourists.

Monumental staircase and pergola. *The pergola and monumental staircase have been listed as historic monuments since December 14, 1989. Initially this staircase, built between 1925 and 1927, climbed up to the Rocher du Drapeau, where the French flag flew. But today only the "Escalier du Centre" remains along with the steps leading to the Rayol beach that runs east to west, split in half by the steps. The main part of the staircase, built from stone from the quarries in the district of Rayol-Canadel, provided residents with access to the beach, since at that time there were no other roads.*

Mediterranean gardens. *The estate is open daily from January 31 to November 20. Founded in 1910 by a colonial explorer, then bought at the start of the Second World War by the famous aeronautical constructor, Henry Potez, only to be later abandoned for many years, the Rayol estate was bought in 1989 by the National Coastal Conservancy.*

Since then, the estate's gardens (20 hectares) have been restored and display flora from Mediterranean climate zones around the world. Californian, Chilean, South African and Australian gardens can all be seen, and a visit to this park will provide an introduction to some surprising natural environments.

Daily guided tours (lasting 1 1/2 hours) provide more information about the plant world and man's use of plants. In summer, the visit includes discovery of the marine environment. Wearing a wetsuit, flippers, mask and snorkel, you can dive into the transparent waters of the Baie du Figuier and learn to identify the main marine animals found along the coastal fringe. In July and August, musical evenings are held every Monday night in the gardens.

Les Jardins du Domaine du Rayol, avenue des Belges, 83820 Le Rayol-Canadel. Tel. 04 94 05 32.

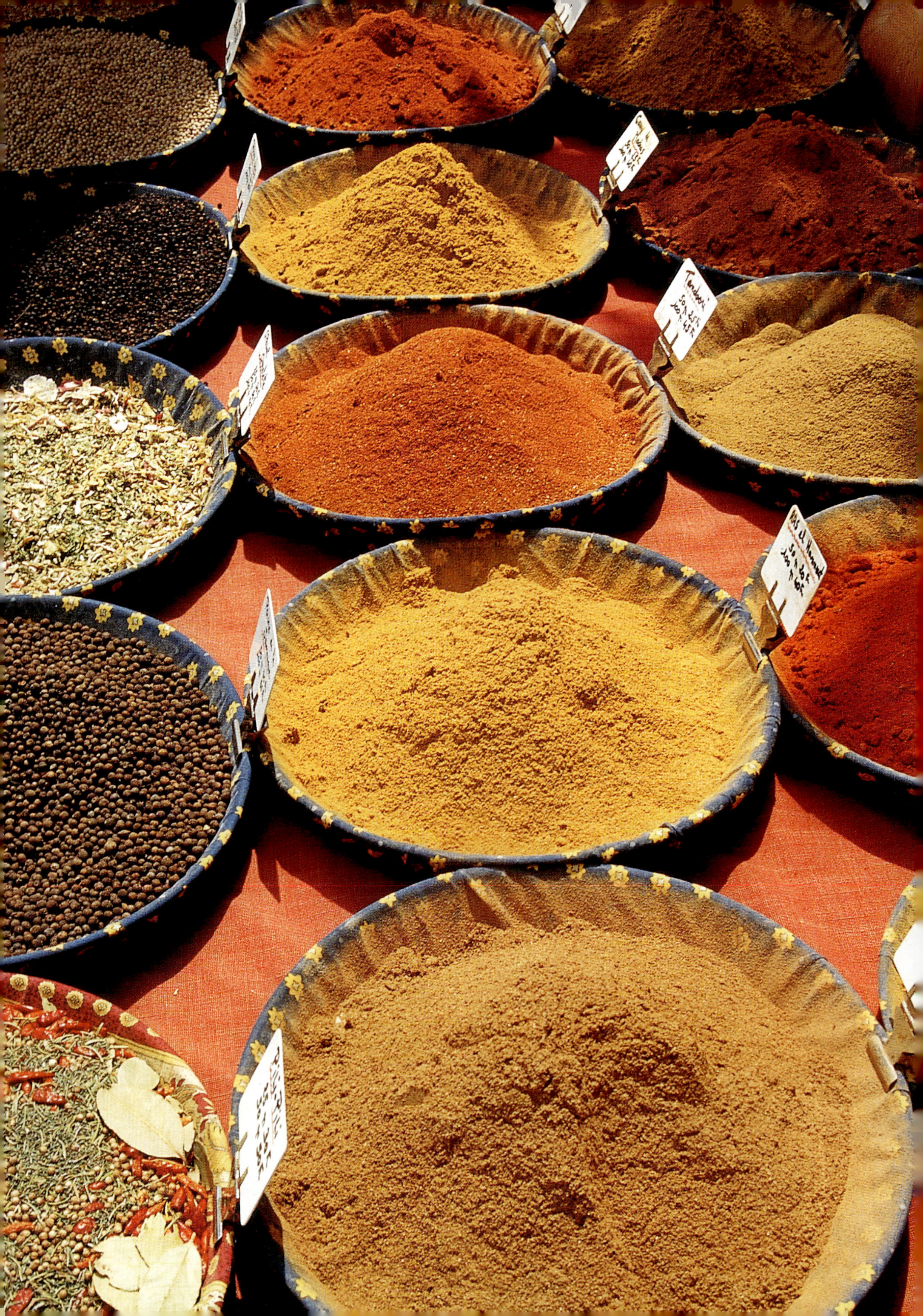

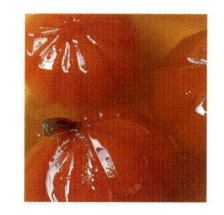

Tastes, scents and products of the Riveria

Cooking here is done using olive oil and delicate herbs and spices. Pastis is drunk at an outdoor café in the company of friends. Italy is just down the road and shares the same roots, the same loves and the same definition of happiness.

Recent studies suggest that the life expectancy of those living in the South of Europe is eleven years longer than that of their counterparts in the North, and the suicide rate is half as low.

These same studies put forward a range of theories to explain this greater longevity, this eagerness to keep on living.

One of the theories is of course the quality of life, the diet and also the rhythm of day-to-day life.

The Mediterranean: a window of light.

[...] Let night fall, let the hours go by, the days pass on and here stand I...
(G. Apollinaire.)

Right:
By mid-April, the French Riviera is dotted with poppies, whilst in Paris the chestnut trees are only just blossoming. (photo E. Cattin).

The art of pétanque.

Another curious fact is that there are more doctors here than in other regions and yet there is less demand for them. Clearly then, doctors, like ourselves, like to enjoy the good life, and in the sunshine if at all possible!

But perhaps it is the sun itself that keeps us hanging on to life, enjoying life no matter what.

And perhaps all the rest - the warm air, the evening scent of jasmine, the shimmering firefly, the smell of freshly cut grass, sitting down in the shade to eat stuffed vegetables with your hands, and the inexpressible pleasure of taking a siesta in the dense afternoon silence – perhaps all of this is just a result of that sunshine.

Is it all just because the sun, that sovereign god, generously doles out life in long and happy doses?

It is all thanks to the sun. The glass of chilled wine when you are really thirsty, the shade of an olive tree, the taste of fruit, the joyful cries at the market... It only exists because the sun is there, day after day, pale in winter, bright in autumn, peaceful and calm in spring and in summer.

PASTIS

The recipe is simple. One measure of milky liquid for five measures of water. Pastis is a drink that is synonymous with sunshine, and seems to fascinate teenagers when served as a "perroquet" with a shot of mint, or with just a hint of orgeat to charm the ladies. Served at its most simple, the clink of ice and those little drops of liquid on the glass are enough to cast their cloudy spell upon us.

This is nectar from paradise, pure satisfaction that makes you beg for more, the finest and most luxurious way to quench one's thirst.

The different forms of pastis are made from a mixture of alcohol concentrated at 96.3%: essence of aniseed, essence of star aniseed obtained from distillation, liquorice powder, water, sugar and the infusion of several plants, the proportions of which are a closely guarded secret. This preparation is left to macerate for two to three weeks and is then filtered and tested before being bottled.

THE OLIVE TREE

It was the sacred olive tree that was the first to emerge from the flood as a sign to Noah that the punishment was over and that life on earth could begin once again.

In Rome, it was Minerva, Goddess of wisdom, who taught men the art of growing olive trees.

It is indeed a sacred tree. In popular belief as in the main monotheist religions, anointing is a symbol of the link between man and God, and the oil obtained from this legendary tree is held sacred by the Catholic religion. Its branches are used to decorate churches on Palm Sunday. Holy oils are still used today to ordain priests and for the holy sacraments, from baptisms to the extreme unction.

The olive harvest begins in September with the green olives, whilst the black ones continue to ripen throughout October. Those olives that are destined to be pressed are only harvested in December, although timing can vary from one area to another depending on the climate.

Harvesting techniques vary too, according to the use and purity of the oil one wishes to obtain. Manual harvesting is by far the best since the fruit is not damaged by nets or when falling, and does not develop mould which could subsequently alter the oil's acidity. Today though, for ease of harvest, a long toothed comb is usually run through the branches to gather the fruit.

It takes 5 kilograms of olives to make 1 litre of oil, and a good harvester can harvest about ninety kilos per day.

The method used to extract the oil is more than six thousand years old, and olive oil has always been extracted using the simple methods that were still in use in 19th century Syria. The olives were first crushed in a mortar and the paste was placed in an earthenware jar. Hot water was then added and kneaded in by hand. The oil, being lighter than water, would rise to the surface.

Today, after sorting, the olives are washed in cold water to remove impurities, then ground in a millstone complete with their stones. The thick paste is thinned and smoothed by kneading. It is then divided into 5 or 6 kilo *"scourtins"* or flat baskets, which are stacked on top of each other. Lastly, it is placed under hydraulic pressure to extract the long-awaited liquid from the olive. This is what is known as virgin, first cold pressed, olive oil. The oil is then decanted by centrifugation. Its appearance, taste and acidity are tested, and any second-class oils are sent for refining and used in soap making.

FRENCH RIVIERA

Olive oil and health

Recent studies have shown that the Mediterranean diet encourages lower rates of heart disease, and olive oil is particularly healthy.
It does not modify gastric acidity in the stomach, it helps the liver and gall bladder by encouraging the slow but regular transit of bile to the intestine, allowing the liver to rest; and it does not modify the cholesterol content of the bile.
It eases digestion and protects veins and arteries thanks to the high levels of anti-oxidizing Vitamin E. It thins the blood, preventing thrombosis, and reduces the likelihood of arteriosclerosis.
And this miracle oil even allows us to think straight, protecting the brain against ageing, toxins and viruses.

Olive oil leaves you glowing with health.

Freshly harvested olives are bitter and hard (photo E. Cattin).

HERBS
One cannot conceive of the French Riviera's cuisine without the use of a wide variety of herbs and condiments, the very symbols of sunshine.
Local products make the perfect match for these herbs, which can be used either fresh or dried.

Basil
An annual plant, sold all summer long in the local markets in bunches or in small pots. Basil leaves can be small or large, and should be used fresh since they lose their flavour when dried and do not freeze well. Basil is widely used here, and takes pride of place in "soupe au pistou", although it is also used in salads, meats, pasta and various sauces.

Pan-bagnat
This is the ultimate Niçois sandwich with the distinctly Mediterranean taste of olives and olive oil.
Preparation
Cut a large roll in half horizontally and sprinkle the inside with olive oil. Cover the bottom half with desalted anchovies, thinly sliced tomatoes, sliced onion, thin slices of green pepper, and garnish with small black olives after removing their stones. Add a dash of olive oil, cover with the other half of the roll, and enjoy.

(Photo Didier Benaouda)

Soupe au pistou

"Pistou" comes from the Latin *"pistare"*, which means *"to crush"*, since the basil leaves must be crushed in a mortar to be used in this recipe. Pistou is like a ray of sunshine in your cooking, and can be spread on bread, used to season pasta or vegetable soups, or to bring out the taste of steamed vegetables, grilled fish etc. A descendant of the herb soups of the Middle Ages, soupe au pistou is similar to Italian minestrone, full of vegetables and sunshine. Some even say that this traditional Provençal recipe was invented by a duchess to seduce a marquis during an intimate little dinner that took place in the 18th century.

Preparation time: 15 minutes
Cooking time: approx. 1 hour
Ingredients
   500g red kidney beans
   500g haricot beans
   125g mange tout, strings removed
   250g small courgettes, diced
   250g small red and yellow broad beans
   a few tablespoons of pistou
   salt and pepper
   250g of very ripe, peeled tomatoes
   100g cooked pasta of your choice (e.g. small macaroni)

Preparation
Place all the vegetables in a pot, cover with cold water and bring to the boil. Lower the heat, add salt and pepper, cover and leave to simmer for at least one hour. Meanwhile, prepare the pistou (see recipe). When the vegetables are well cooked, add the pasta and cook until tender (about twenty minutes). Serve the soup in a soup dish with the pistou and grated Parmesan cheese.

Preparing the pistou:
Crush 250 ml of basil in a mortar with three cloves of garlic. Add a trickle of olive oil to reduce the mixture to a paste. Add a little grated Gruyere cheese.

Anchoïade

Ingredients
   2 cloves of garlic, finely minced
   2 tablespoons of olive oil
   60 anchovy fillets in oil
   1 tablespoon snipped parsley
   1 tablespoon snipped basil
   half a lemon
   3 egg yolks

Preparation
Place all the ingredients in a small saucepan, with the exception of the lemon juice and egg yolks. Leaver to simmer and melt on a low heat for 15 minutes, whilst stirring. Beat the egg yolks with the lemon juice. Pour into the mixture and thicken on a low heat, stirring constantly. Remove from heat. Add a few grinds of pepper. Serve warm with garlic croutons and raw vegetables.

Once the bud is removed, garlic has excellent properties.

Ideal for a refreshing herbal drink or delicious roasts.

Rosemary

A native of the Mediterranean basin, the Roman name for this little shrub means "sea dew". It is one of the South of France's finest plants, with its long stems, always green, and pale blue flowers. The herb is very strong and must be used with skill to avoid becoming too dominant. When soaked in oil, it gives off a discreet aroma, and once trimmed, its branches can be used as skewers. Excellent for grilled meats, which can be brushed with oil using rosemary twigs as brushes.

Bay leaves

The bay tree is an evergreen shrub, which in the wild can grow up to 10 metres high. It is a key ingredient in the kitchen, and the leaves are often ground to a powder to be more easily diluted. Whole, the leaves can be used in marinades, stock, stews and ratatouille.

Thyme

Another native of the Mediterranean, thyme, so legend has it, is one of the beautiful Helen's tears, which the Gods transformed into a generous, perfumed herb. It is a perennial that grows in compact, rounded clumps that have many branches. This little grey coloured shrub with tiny leaves and strongly scented sap, has an aroma that varies according to the variety of plant. It is one of the sun-baked plants that cover the region's arid hillsides. Gathered just before it flowers, which it does between April and September, thyme can be used in many preparations and in all kinds of dishes: grilled meats, marinades and salads.

Sage

Sage is a small bush-like tree with branches of between 30 and 60 centimetres. Its leaves are greyish and downy and are used in cooking, although they should not be used in combination with other herbs. Used to flavour mutton stew, roast pork and even wine.

Chives

Chives grow in clumps and are a perennial plant. The fine, dark green stems are cylindrical, hollow and thick. Chives are particularly appreciated in the South of France, and can be chopped and added to tomato salads for example. This is one of the ingredients in mixed herbs.

Marjoram or oregano

This perennial, originating in Asia Minor, is extremely aromatic and much used. It is a marvellous herb for tomato coulis, pizzas, stuffings and vinaigrettes.

Wild thyme

This climbing plant, similar to thyme, has small pointed leaves. It grows mainly on arid ground on dry, rocky hillsides. It is a delicious herb that can be used with mutton, stews, sauces and marinades.

Other plants, like lavender and lemon verbena, also make excellent herbal teas.

SPECIALITIES OF THE SEA

The rich resources of the "big blue", Mediterranean fish, crustaceans and shellfish, are an integral part of culinary traditions on the French Riviera. The local cuisine has some perfect recipes for preparing Mediterranean seafood using olive oil, garlic and fennel.

Bream is an excellent fish that can be enjoyed whole or in fillets, grilled, cooked in a court bouillon, or baked.

Another much appreciated fish when grilled or oven-baked is the white sea bream.

The scorpion fish, a fundamental part of local cuisine
(photo E. Cattin).

Red mullet, and especially striped red mullet, is one of the most highly esteemed fish in the Mediterranean. It can be grilled, fried or baked, but should not be either poached or steamed.

Wrasse, which often have an orange stripe, are mainly used in fish soups. They can also be used in bouillabaisse.

As for scorpion fish, these are irreplaceable in bouillabaisse and remain one of the most prestigious symbols of all Mediterranean fish.

Sole à la Provençale (fried with tomatoes, aubergines and mixed herbs) is delicious. Sardines are excellent either fresh (grilled, fried or baked) or tinned.

Crustaceans such as the velvet swimming crab or the locust lobster are a delicious addition to bouillabaisse and fish soup. Another much appreciated shellfish here is known as *"violet"*.

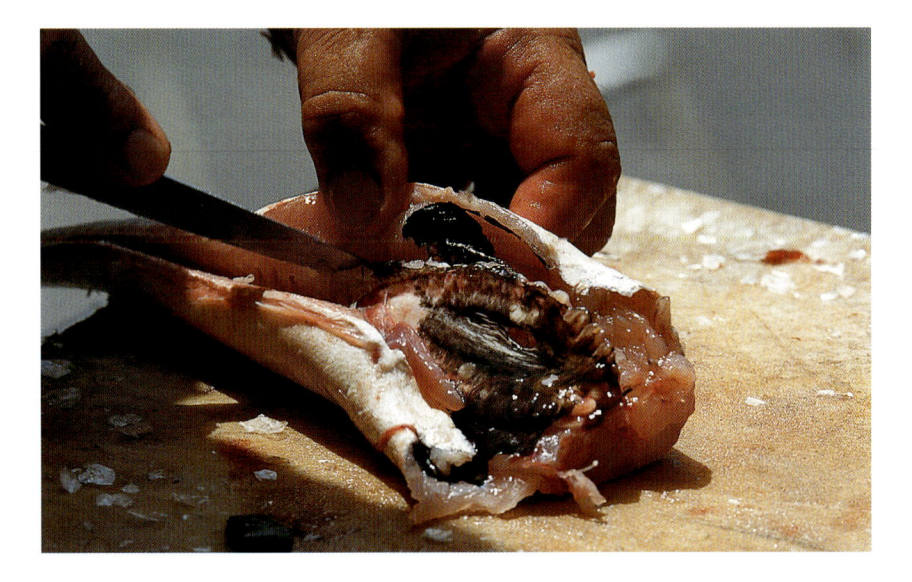

At the market, fish is handled roughly but skilfully.

If you're dreaming of a simple life, eating grilled fish on the beach...no need to go as far as the tropics!

Walking around the capes
Part of the pleasure of the Riviera is to flush out a scent of seaweed mixed with resin and honeysuckle along the coastal footpaths around the capes.
Cap d'Antibes: 2 kilometres there and back on a well-marked footpath bordered with Aleppo pine, taking you to the southern tip of the peninsula that lies between Antibes and Juan-les-Pins, and to the sanctuary of Notre-Dame-de-la-Garoupe.
Cap Ferrat: you can walk around this "millionaires' peninsula" along an 11 kilometre footpath taking in the Pointe Saint-Hospice. Another footpath links Lilong to the Passable beach, and one can walk to the port of Saint-Jean by the Chemin du Roy that goes past the former property of King Léopold II of Belgium. Coves, limestone cliffs and Mediterranean trees line this superb coastal walk.
Cap Martin: follow in Nietzsche's footsteps along the "Le Corbusier" footpath and discover the "cabanon" along the way. Broom, myrtle, pistachio trees and lentisks line the footpath that continues all the way to the beach at Monaco.
Cap d'Ail: a coastal footpath linking the Mala beach to the Marquet beach in an hour long walk along the cliffs of Cap Rognoso and the Pointe des Douaniers.

(Photo E. Cattin)

planting better vines and astutely blending different grapes. The *"rosés de saignée"* are the best of all, with their aroma of rosemary and lavender. Some of the "dry" *muscat* wines are also well worth tasting. The rosés of this region are thus breaking away from their classification as table wines and becoming a respected and well-promoted product. Bellet, grown in the hills around Nice, is a wine that is made from only 40 hectares of vines.

Wine-growing can also be found in Porquerolles, where two private estates produce two remarkable wines: the Domaine de l'Ile and Domaine de la Courtade. The first, about thirty hectares, was the first vineyard to obtain the *"appellation contrôlée"* (AOC Côtes de Provence) and its reputation is now firmly established. As for the Domaine de la Courtade, its aims to create a high-quality vineyard with a low yield, and hopes to earn the new *"appellation"* Porquerolles in the not too distant future.

WINES

Although the wine-making prestige of the French Riviera cannot compare with that of the Bordeaux region or the Côte du Rhône, a new philosophy of quality rather than quantity is currently raising the reputation of these often delicious wines. This is especially the case of rosé wines. Many estates in the Var are concentrating on this type of production. But what used to be nothing more than a refreshing wine to accompany a summer barbecue is today becoming a wine of complex aromas, perfectly suitable for more sophisticated uses. All of this is to the wine producers' merit, since they are

Dusty bottles in the wine cellar at the Château de la Chèvre d'Or.

61

Here, cooking is like poetry... Dried rose buds blended with finely ground black pepper give an unbeatable taste to grilled meats.

When eaten alone, crystallised fruit can be too sweet for the palate. But try just a small piece, served with its juice in a bowl of yoghurt. Or an apricot with a scoop of almond milk ice cream served in an infusion of star anise... Pleasure is all about combining light and dark.

FRUITS AND FLOWERS, TASTES AND SCENTS

Tourrettes-sur-Loup: food for the fairies

At the Florian confectionery factory at Tourettes-sur-Loup, you can taste rose petals, violet flowers and crystallised jasmine, as well as rose and jasmine jams.

Eze: concentrated happiness

Here, the Fragonard boutique is a riot of colour, tastes, textures and atmosphere, a blend of all the marvellous scents of the Mediterranean, just as you always dreamed of.

One of the most amusing and allusive essences of all

Crystallised fruit

These golden citrus fruits - oranges, mandarins, clementines and lemons - are found in all the gardens of the area and, when transformed into the crystallised fruit that is also found all over the French Riviera (often in basket presentations), are a feast both for the eyes and the palate.

TASTES, SCENTS AND PRODUCTS OF THE RIVIERA

is called "La Sieste": a blend of vetiver, with rockrose, musk and cinnamon leaves, to caress the defenceless skin of a sleeping man.

Precious perfumes in golden vials, refined *eaux de parfums* and lighter *eaux de toilette*. Fragonard's fragrances are full of sunshine, with names like "Grain de Soleil" or "Harmonie de Jasmin", perfumed with orange flower, freesia, lily and rose, syringa, wisteria, iris and blackcurrant buds, amber, sandalwood and musk, or white flowers and green herbs.

Here you can rediscover the joys of soap made the old-fashioned way and from the best ingredients, crafted using authentic traditions.

Chard

Chard, known here as "blette", seems to have truly found a place for itself on the French Riviera. It adds flavour to minced meats and stuffings, and has also found a rather more original use for those with a sweet tooth, in the "tourte de blettes", mixed with fruits and brown sugar and baked in puff pastry.

Left: **The spring rose harvest at the Fragonard factory** (Fragonard).

A little taste of hell in heaven: pepper and figs

Here there is a variety of fig called the "drop of gold", visually striking when ripe, dripping with amber juice. In the 18th century, it was a custom to take three very ripe fruits and spread them on a slice of wheat bread, then add a grind of pepper to bring out the smoothness of the flavour.

Courgette flowers in batter

Serves 6.
Select about forty courgette flowers, either at the market or pick them yourself.
1 bunch of parsley, 150g flour, 2 whole eggs, 25 cl cold milk, salt, pepper.
Clean the flowers by removing the stem and pistil and set aside in a bowl. Combine the flour with two egg yolks, a pinch of salt and a teaspoon of olive oil, then add the milk little by little. Whisk the egg whites and add them to the mixture along with the chopped parsley. Add salt and pepper. Soak the flowers one after another in the batter, then immerse in hot frying oil. When golden, lay in a dish lined with kitchen roll.
This dish should be eaten warm.

(Photo E. Cattin.)

TRADITIONAL MARKETS

Farmers from the surrounding countryside, fishermen, fruit and vegetable merchants, flower growers and craftsmen can all be found at the French Riviera's markets. The following are amongst the most authentic and interesting: the one hundred year old flower market of the Cours Saleya in Nice, the Provençal markets in Antibes, Cagnes-sur-Mer, Cannes and Grasse, the organic farmers' market at Villeneuve-Loubet, and the arts and crafts market in Vence.

TASTES, SCENTS AND PRODUCTS OF THE RIVIERA

NICE

Nice's worldwide reputation for fine cuisine is not just a coincidence as all the essential elements of the French Riviera's cuisine can be found here. *Pan-bagnat*, stuffed vegetables, *panisse*, Niçois tripe and ravioli, *bagna-cauda*, gnocchis.

Nice also offers a wide range of fruits, and the growing season here is long. At the market, the products are

Left: **The market on the Cours Saleya in Nice.**

Socca

At the market in Nice, local farmers sell their products, calling out in the local Niçois language, "nissart". Socca sellers tow this huge, golden chickpea pancake behind a motorbike, on a trailer covered with a zinc lid that keeps the trays of socca warm inside. In bars around town, slices of socca are served with a glass of chilled rosé at a wooden table. Socca is very popular in Italy and near Menton, where it is known as "picha". Socca makes a welcome mid-morning snack for early risers, or can be enjoyed around town at any time of the day.

Ingredients
50 cl water
250g chick pea flour
2 + 1 tablespoons of olive oil
salt

Preparation
Make the batter by combining the water, 1 tablespoon of oil, flour and salt. Whisk well to remove all lumps. Roll out in a thin layer on a tray or a tin-plated copper pie dish oiled with olive oil. Leave to rest for a few minutes, then bake in a very hot wood oven or grill on a high heat. Burst any bubbles with a fork as soon as they form. Remove from the oven as soon as it is golden, even if slightly burnt. Sprinkle with pepper. Cut into squares and serve hot.

FRENCH RIVIERA

Salade niçoise - Salada nissarda

This is a traditional dish containing only raw vegetables and hard-boiled eggs. The salad is made without vinegar, by salting the tomatoes and sprinkling them with olive oil. The broad beans, or "févette", are chosen very young to be eaten raw.

Preparation time: 15 minutes

Ingredients for 4 people:
4 tomatoes, quartered and sprinkled with salt
1 small cucumber
150g fresh broad beans
2 green sweet peppers with seeds removed
1 clove garlic, peeled and sliced in half
4 small fresh onions, chopped
2 boiled eggs, quartered, + 1 for the sauce
olive oil
70g Niçois olives
8 anchovy fillets in oil (if the anchovies are salted, soak for 30 minutes in water, changing water regularly, to remove salt)
salt, pepper, basil

Preparation
Peel the cucumber by removing every other strip of skin lengthwise.
Chop finely. Remove as many bones as possible from the anchovies. Chop into four or five pieces. Remove the white core and seeds from the peppers, and slice into fine rings. Remove the skin of the small broad beans. Rub the bottom and sides of the salad bowl with the garlic clove. Crush and chop the remainder.
Place all the vegetables in the salad bowl along with the chopped garlic. Prepare the sauce by mixing the olive oil with the egg yolk. Season with pepper (no salt).
Pour sauce on the vegetables.
Add the black olives.
Chill for 30 minutes before serving.

The Cours Saleya
Breathe in the scents of the fruit and vegetable market on the Cours Saleya, where local producers sing out about their products in the Niçois language. This is the region of fennel, little red cloves of garlic, rosemary, thyme and wild thyme, marjoram and farigoulette *(which adds a colourful taste to local specialities)*. And of course this is the region of basil, or "ballico" *as it is known here,* which is used in making pistou.

Recipe for stuffed vegetables, "petit farcis nicois", by Jacques Maximin

Basil butter
Ingredients for 6 people:
6 purple artichokes
50 g tomatoes
6 new white onions, to be stuffed
6 round Niçois courgettes
500g of beef, cooked in a pot-au-feu with vegetables (carrots and onions)
200g fresh breadcrumbs soaked in the stock from the pot-au-feu
salt, pepper
allspice
2 chopped shallots
chopped parsley
white wine
grated parmesan cheese
50cl stock
150g fresh butter
1 or 2 bunches of fresh chopped basil
and a sufficient quantity of olive oil.

(Photo D. Benaouda.)

The recipe:

The vegetables: cut the lid off
the top of the courgettes and onions.
Scoop out the insides, then steam or boil,
being sure that they remain firm. Cool and
drain. Set aside the insides of the vegetables.
Turn the purple artichokes, hollow slightly,
and braise.
Hull the tomatoes. Peel them without removing
the stalks, then cut a lid off them and empty
them carefully. Salt slightly and turn
them over to drain.
The stuffing: the leftovers from a pot-au-feu are
perfect for this stuffing. Soak the breadcrumbs
in the hot beef stock.
Stir-fry the meat (for example chuck steak)
with a little garlic, along with the vegetables
(carrots, onions) and the flesh from
the emptied vegetables. Put this mixture
through a fine mincer then mix the minced
meat, vegetables and soaked breadcrumbs
together. Season to taste with salt, pepper,
allspice, Cayenne pepper, two chopped shallots,
parsley, white wine and grated parmesan.
Stuff all the small vegetables and place
them in an ovenproof dish. Sprinkle with a
ladle-full of stock, season, add olive oil,
crushed garlic clove and a branch of thyme.
Braise slowly in a medium oven (160o) firstly
with a protective cover, then remove
the cover to glaze the stuffed vegetables.
Check that they are cooked then set
to one side on the edge of the baking tray.
To finish: reduce the remaining stock and
season to taste. When serving, sprinkle
with hot butter and chopped garlic,
and add a grind of pepper and a trickle
of olive oil.
686, chemin de la Gaude -
06140 Vence -
Tel. 04 93 58 90 75.

all fresh and full of sunshine. Nice is the only city to boast a vintage wine with an *"appellation contrôlée"*, and also the oldest variety of grape in the world: the *vin de Bellet* (red, white and rosé).

Nice also specialises in preparing and serving fish, often cooked in a saffron-coloured stock

Another speciality, stockfish, is a dried fish of Scandinavian origin. This is a type of haddock, dried in the sun and snows of Norway, which Northern sailors would use to barter with when they entered a port of call. With time, it has become a genuine Niçois dish, and the "estocafic" once made in Norway using dairy products has become a delicate tomato stew called "estocaficada", cooked in a casserole dish with olive oil, potato, garlic and peppers.

French marigolds.

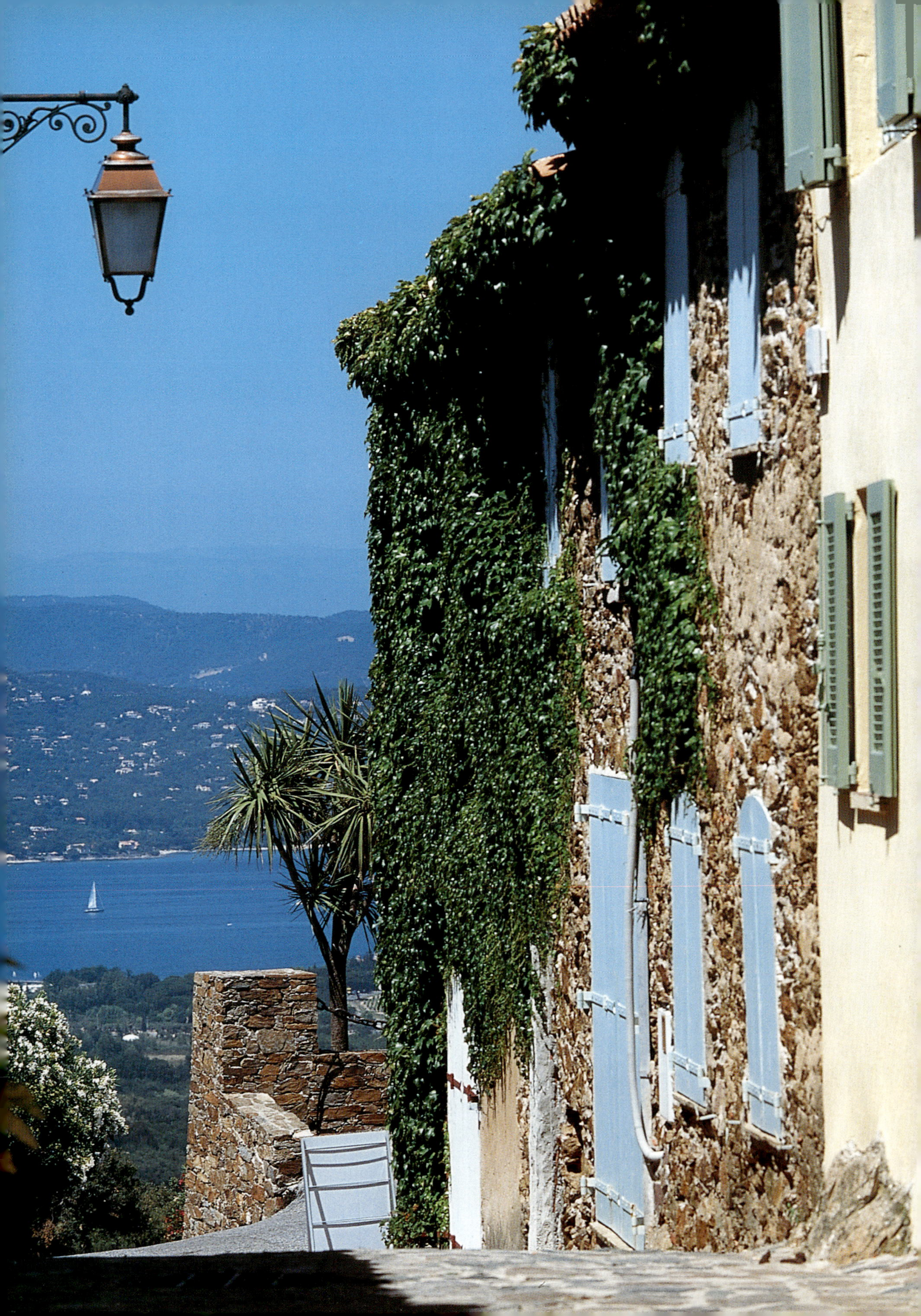

Perched villages

Gorbio
Sainte-Agnès
Roquebrune
Peille
Peillon
La Turbie
Eze
Saint-Paul
Vence
Tourettes-sur-Loup
Gourdon
Biot
Mougins
Ramatuelle
Gassin
Grimaud
Collobrières
Chartreuse de la Verne
Bormes-les-Mimosas

For centuries, only the hardiest travellers would venture upon journeys that were slow, long and perilous, and only for the most exceptional reasons. Forced by war, or for commercial reasons, only a rare few would take to the roads, and it would have seemed very strange indeed to find it enjoyable. And yet, in the 18th century, a few eccentrics began to travel, looking for something new and exotic that they

Left: ***The dazzling village of Gassin.***

The houses in Peillon seem to cling to the steeple.

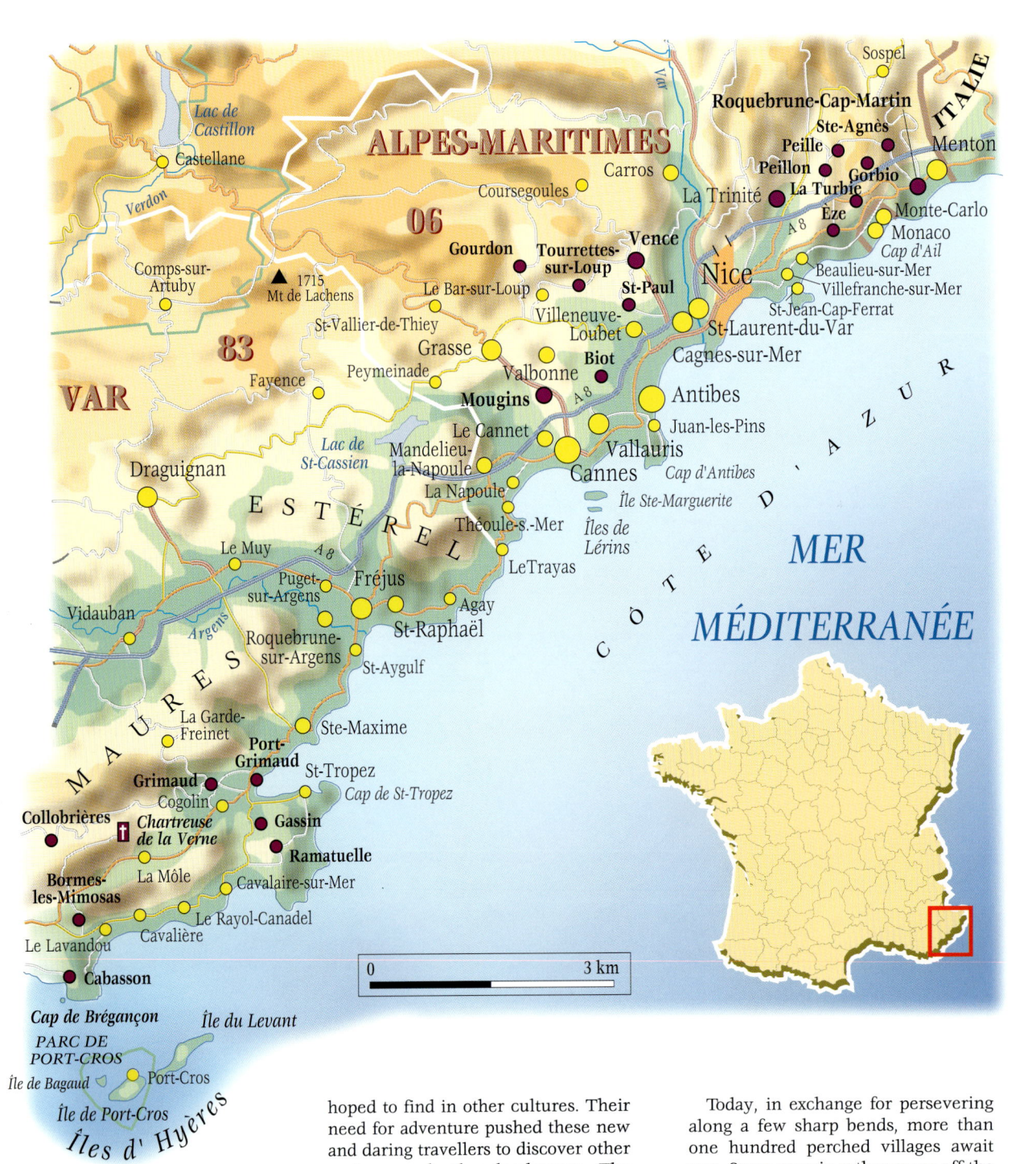

hoped to find in other cultures. Their need for adventure pushed these new and daring travellers to discover other customs and other landscapes. The steep perched villages of the Riviera, which until then had remained unvisited due to their inaccessibility, became a prized destination for these first tourists. The villages were indeed a rare commodity since they were so difficult to get to.

Today, in exchange for persevering along a few sharp bends, more than one hundred perched villages await you. Some remain rather more off the beaten track than others. Even the most famous ones have been able to conserve their carefully concealed charm, though they only reveal it to those who know where to look for it at the right time, either very early or very late in the day.

GORBIO

8 kilometres above Roquebrune, this medieval village sits beneath the imposing Mont Agel, at 360 metres above sea level, in a grandiose setting between the wild summits of the Cime de Gorbio and the Cime de Briançon and the Col de Madone. The village's steep streets are home to some magnificent old houses, 11th and 17th century gateways, charming little squares where the silence is barely broken by the murmur of old fountains. In these little streets with their medieval covered passages, cascading flowers and old stones full of history, there are many cultural events in the summer months: musical evenings, the cherry festival in June and the amazing *"procession des limaces"*, which although the name means "procession of slugs" is actually a succession of empty snails shells lit with flames. Of note here are the ruins of the Château des Lascaris with its 13th century defence tower, and the 19th century château of the Counts Alziari de Malaussène. Also, the Saint Barthélemy's church dating back to 1663, the Chapelle des Penitents Blancs (1445), the 17th century chapel of Saint-Lazare and the 18th century chapel of Saint Roch.

Gorbio, on the way to the Serre de la Madone.

The setting sun paints its colours across the road from Sainte-Agnès to Peille.

SAINTE-AGNÈS

This is the highest coastal village in Europe. From its standpoint at 760 metres above sea level, Sainte-Agnès offers a breathtaking 1800 view of the sea, with Menton below, the northern Alps behind, and Italy in the distance, lost in a sea of blue.

This is one of the most beautiful villages in France, definitely a case of love at first sight!

It is formed by one long, straight road and a tangle of little cobbled streets, small squares and vaulted alleyways. Don't miss the 17th century church of Notre-Dame-des-Neiges with its hundred-year-old lime trees, the chapel of Saint-Sébastien below the village, the ruins of the feudal castle, and the medieval garden at the foot of the lower village wall. The viewpoint diagram on the highest rock overlooking the village is definitely of interest and provides a great excuse for a walk up there. The reward once you reach the top makes all the effort more than worthwhile.

On the way back down, you can always stop at the café-restaurant at the entrance to the village. It is simple and traditional, with one of the nicest terraces on the Riviera.

The Sainte-Agnès fort on the outskirts of the village was built between 1932 and 1938 and was an important part of the Maginot line.

Sainte-Agnès, a charming village overlooking Menton.

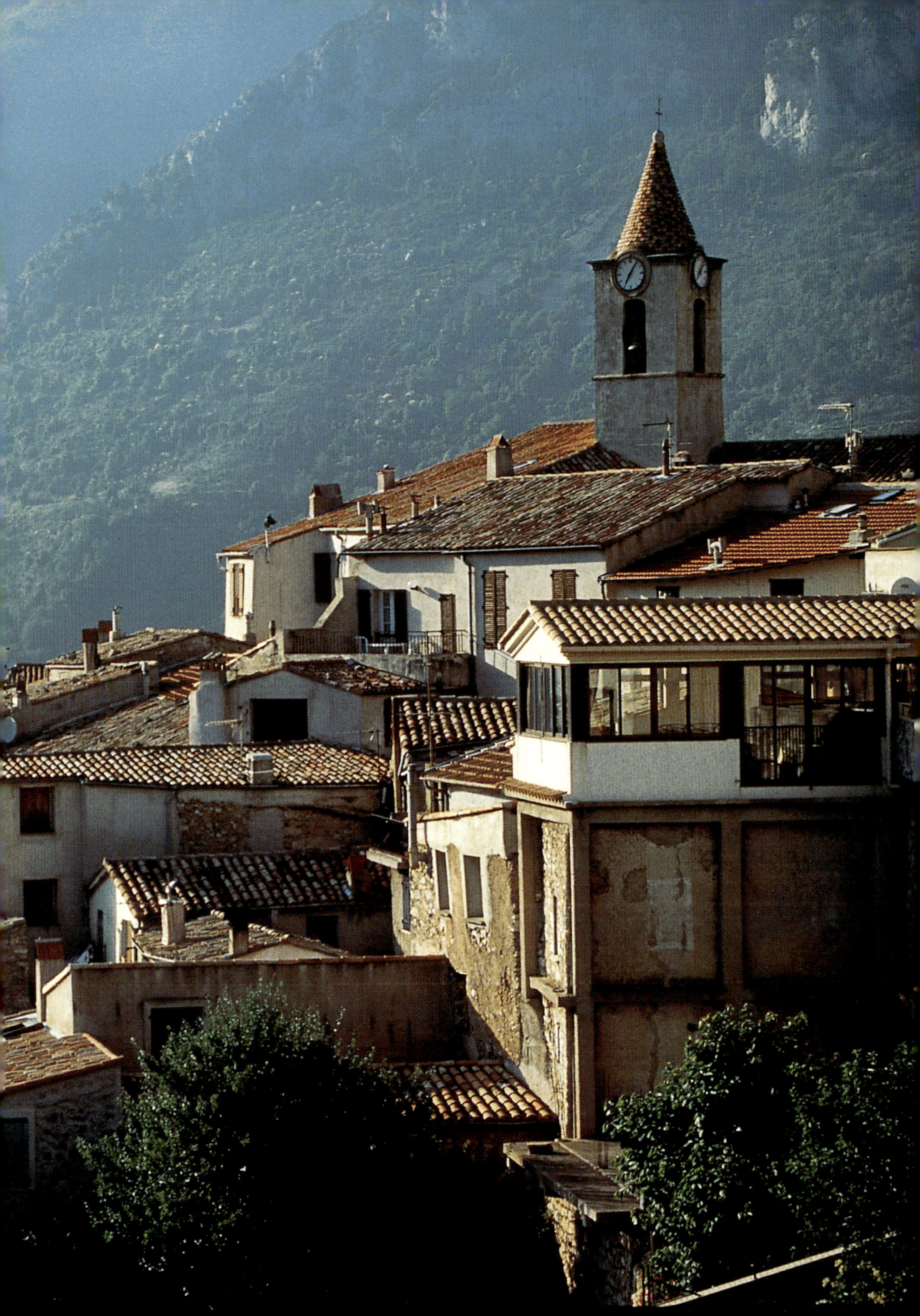

Closed shutters at siesta time.

ROQUEBRUNE

The district of Roquebrune, between Monaco and Menton, stretches all the way up to the old village with its castle. This remarkable site offers a captivating panoramic view of the mountains and Monte-Carlo.

A walk around the old village is a must, with its 10th century castle and dungeon, the church of Sainte-Marguerite, its thousand year old olive tree and the rue Montcollet. Also, the procession of August 5th, a tradition dating back five centuries and reproducing scenes from the Passion. It is also worth taking the tourist route around Cap Martin to enjoy the pine forests, mimosa, cypress and olive groves.

PEILLE

15 kilometres north of Monaco, Peille is a superb little medieval village clinging on to the side of a mountain, surrounded by the summits of Mont Agel, the Pic de Baudon and the Cime de Rastel behind Monaco and Menton. Step through the old gateway to the village, located at the foot of the

Open shutters with flowers.

rock, into a world of beautiful little old squares, gothic fountains, large medieval-style houses, narrow cobbled streets and magnificent restored chapels. Peille's ruined fortifications bear witness to its distant but glorious past, as do the 14th century courthouse (the Palais des Consuls) and the robust Palais des Lascaris built in the 14th century on the edge of a cliff. The viewpoint offers a wonderful panoramic view over maritime pine and oak forests. Also of note: the 12th century church of Sainte-Marie; the chapel of Saint-Sébastien (13th century); the Chapelle de la Miséricorde - a mill for pressing olive oil; the chapel of Saint-Joseph (18th century); as well as prehistoric and archaeological remains. For the more energetic visitors, the Via Ferrata is a specially adapted climbing site, suitable even for novices and with a superb view of the village.

Peillon's fountain is a listed monument.

PEILLON

The whole of this magnificent medieval fortified village is listed as an historic monument. It stands like an eyrie on a sheer cliff, and this is definitely the place where the word "perched" comes into its own! Peillon - overlooking the Paillon de l'Escarène valley - is truly a journey into the past, with its winding streets intersected by vaulted alleyways and wide stairways. The tall old houses with their ancient wooden doors and the faded golden colours of the old walls are truly enchanting. Of note: the Chapelle des

Principality of Monaco. It is a large and charming village with its "calades" (streets cobbled with pebbles) and flower-boxes, medieval vaulted alleyways, old houses tastefully restored and little shaded squares, all bearing witness the village's past. Whatever you do, don't miss the incomparable view of the Gulf of Ventimiglia in Italy, the Cap Martin, Cap Ferrat, Cap de Nice, Antibes and all the way to the Esterel. Also of note, the medieval walls, the 18th century church of Saint-Michel, an historic monument, the vaulted porches and the monumental fountain of 1824.

Pénitents Blancs, 1495, the church of the Transfiguration, 18th century, the oil and flour mills, and the Roman road leading to Peille, a two hour walk away.

LA TURBIE

The village is famous for its "Trophée des Alpes" or "Trophée d'Auguste", a genuine masterpiece of Roman art, a uniquely superb 35-metre high tower dating from 6 BC. La Turbie stands at 1150 metres above sea level, at the Tête de Chien on the upper coastal road overlooking the

Notre-Dame-de-Laghet
A "feeling that life is stronger than death", wrote Guillaume Apollinaire, deeply moved by the countless plaques of thanks that cover the cloister walls of Notre-Dame-de-Laghet: "The meticulous, awe-filled awkwardness of the primitive art that predominates here is enough to touch even an unbeliever.
All possible types of accident, fatal illness, pain and human misery are depicted here, naively, devotedly and ingeniously..."

"The sea is angry and full of white horses... The ship speeds onwards but is impossible to manoeuvre... The men's gestures show that they know they are condemned. Unless the Virgin intervenes, they will be lost."
(Extract from the work "Ex-voto marins", published by Ouest France, 1996).

Èze.

EZE

Step through the village gate at 390 metres above sea level and discover this small and charming Provençal village, overflowing with flowers and surrounded by luscious vegetation...banana trees, date trees, carob trees, orange and lemon trees...

Eze stretches all the way from Cap Roux at sea level up to the Pointe de Cabuel summit. Eze's history is fully present in the narrow streets of the old medieval village. The two watch towers at the entrance to the village, the postern and arrow slit are all listed as historic monuments.

A footpath - a one hour walk - leads to the superb gardens of the Château de la Chèvre-d'Or.

From there, one can walk down to "Eze bord de mer" at sea level, via the Friedrich Nietzsche footpath (at the end of the Avenue du Jardin Exotique). Here, under the pine and olive trees, Nietzsche is said to have been inspired to write the last part of "Thus spoke Zarathustra".

Of note: the Chapelle des Pénitents Blancs, the parish church and its baroque nave, the cemetery where the

PERCHED VILLAGES

The church at Eze.

Château de la Chèvre-d'Or

This château turned luxury hotel is without doubt one of the most beautiful in the world, almost unbearably so. Located on the cliffs of Eze overlooking the Mediterranean, it stands in a fairytale setting in which luxury blends discreetly with the beauty of the landscape. Everything here is flourishing, refined and subtle, with jasmine terraces, olive and lemon trees thriving in this steep paradise, and rooms with bathrooms that look out over the blue Mediterranean sea. The restaurant deserves not just its three stars, but all those shining in the sky above this garden of Eden.

famous humorist, Francis Blanche, is buried, and the botanical gardens. Visit the Galimard soap factory and the Fort of La Revère (col d'Eze).

Also, don't miss the spice seller just in front of the entrance to the old village, and the Fragonard boutique selling soaps, perfumed candles, honeycomb weave household linen and other delicacies and scents of the south.

(Photo F. Fernandez)

SAINT-PAUL

It is no surprise that famous writers, poets and painters have all chosen to live here. Standing on a rocky spur, surrounded by ramparts built on the orders of François I, Saint-Paul is certainly one of the most beautiful villages in Provence. From the ramparts, there are superb views of the surrounding hills, the coastline and the sea. The scenery here is truly majestic.

The Hôtel de La Colombe d'Or is famous as a place where artists of all times have come to spend a night or a week or so. Modigliani, Soutine, Picasso, Chagall, Miro and Max Ernst all stayed here, as did Gide and Prévert.

"Today, somewhere in La Colombe, with its green almonds, olive branches and citrons, red figs bursting open in the sun, Arcimboldo is painting his portrait. Braque and Léger are watching and giving their opinion, and Villon too, and many others..."

Saint-Paul-de-Vence continues to live up to its reputation as an exceptional site...though perhaps a little too popular, especially on holidays. But then, all you have to do is visit it another day, in another season. Of note: the collegiate church and its treasure

Don't miss the Maeght Foundation at Saint-Paul-de-Vence.

PERCHED VILLAGES

house, the chapel of Saint-Mathieu and the Maeght Foundation, with a major collection of paintings, sculptures, ceramics, drawings and graphic works of the 20th century. Also, the local history museum and the museum of Saint-Paul.

"Saint-Paul is an old beauty, built of bricks, stones and cement, and completely forgotten, except by the sun. White and new, it was built for the violent softness of an Othello, and there is something Moorish about the place. Today, it is the colour of olive trees. It still stands firm and haughty on its base, a hillside surrounded by vineyards, as if the exhilaration of wine itself had carried it up there in a single leap. It is like a wave of stones that has broken on the summit. It is squeezed tightly into a corset of fortified walls. The faded rooftops soak up the sun like a sponge; the walls of the pink and blue houses form a frieze, illustrated by greenery. All of its years are gathered up between the walls of its narrow streets and the cobblestones, scraped by the passing feet of the villagers."
(Franz Hellens, "Notes prises d'une lucarne", 1925)

Dufy, Chagall and D.H. Lawrence, among others, have all lived and dreamed in Vence.

VENCE

"This morning, I was walking in front of my house when I saw young girls, women and men all cycling towards the market. I thought I was in Tahiti."

August 1943. This is how Henri Matisse described Vence, this marvellous village with its narrow streets.

Dufy, Chagall, Dubuffet, Carzon, Arman, Anthony Mars and D.H. Lawrence all lived there, artists constantly trying to find themselves, as they did sometimes in this magic place, only to pick themselves up and fly away again.

Of note: the Château des Villeneuve (17th century), the tower, the Marseillais columns, the cathedral, the Chapelle du Rosaire and the Chapelle des Pénitents Blancs, and the Henri Matisse arts centre. In summer, classical music and jazz concerts. Secondhand book fair.

TOURRETTES-SUR-LOUP

Fortunately, Tourrettes-sur-Loup is a little less well known than the other perched villages of the French Riviera, although it is none the less beautiful. Set a little off that beaten track that tourists tend to rush down desperately clutching at beauty that they never really grasp, Tourrettes-sur-Loup is a charming medieval village worth a long and appreciative look.

PERCHED VILLAGES

Vence.

FRENCH RIVIERA

The Gorges du Loup and the Gourmes waterfall.

Tourettes-sur-Loup, home of crystallised and freshly cut violets.

Perched on a rocky spur 400 m above sea level, in the midst of abundant vegetation, in particular aloe and prickly pear, Tourrettes-sur-Loup's tall grey stone houses stand resolutely within its circular ramparts. The village is known as the "city of violets", flowers that were grown there for nearly a century in the terraced olive groves all around the village, and the tradition is commemorated by a battle of flowers, held on Sundays in early March.

Take time to stroll through the village, sit in the square and quietly admire the Château des Villeneuve (15th century) or wander down the main street, under the door of the watchtower where Poulenc once lived and composed his "Dialogue des Carmélites".

Of note: the Church of Saint-Grégoire (16th century) and Château des Villeneuve with its 11th and 15th century watchtowers.

GOURDON

This village is classed as one of the most beautiful in France, and makes for a most enjoyable visit. The terraced gardens of the château were designed by Le Nôtre, and there is a splendid panoramic view stretching for 80 km over the Gorges du Loup... particularly impressive at sunset, when you feel almost alone.

BIOT

Biot has always been renowned for its pottery, and was an important centre for ceramics in the Middle Ages. This perched village dates from 154 B.C. and overlooks hillsides covered with olive trees, where roses, mimosa and anemones are now grown in green houses.

Enter the village by the Porte des Tines or Porte des Migraniers, and admire the Portugon, the Cul-de-Sac, the Calade des Migraniers, Lei Croûtons, the Rue de la Reguardo lined with gardens, the Place de l'Ariette, the Rondon, the Rue des Orfèvres, the Place de

Make sure you visit Biot with money in your pocket: the handmade pots and glassware are irresistible.

la Catastrophe (a square where two houses collapsed on the evening of June 12th 1898), the ivy-covered square of the Place des Arcades with its beautiful doorways and archways, the steep arched stairways, and sundials.

Of note: the Roman mausoleum of the Chèvre d'Or. The 14th and 15th century arcades on the square; the Château Funel (19th century); the church of Saint Mary Magdalene; the local history museum; the Fernand-Léger museum; the glass museum; six glassworks and several potteries; and the tourist train that takes you around the village.

Notre-Dame-de-Vie

One of the most moving places on the Riviera is the hermitage of Notre-Dame-de-Vie. This sanctuary, close to the estate where Picasso lived not far from Mougins, is stripped of all architectural vanity, fully revealing its noble lines. It is said that the elegance of this large chapel evokes that of some of the Romanesque churches of Tuscany.
Indeed, the cypress trees and rolling hillsides that surround it are very similar to the scenery around Siena.
The chapel is only open on Sundays during services. Below on the right, the Picasso family property is hidden behind a thick forest of pines, oaks and olive trees.

MOUGINS

The post-war years definitely left their mark on this medieval Provençal village, perched at 260 metres above sea level and surrounded by pine and oak forests. It became famous as Picasso's last refuge, at the Domaine de Notre-Dame-de-Vie.

Just 15 minutes from Cannes, Mougins is surrounded by forest - the Valmasque forest park stretches for 427 hectares - and has been able to preserve its environment, and the charm of its narrow streets lined with superb homes and decorated with flowers. Cocteau, Fernand Léger, Paul Eluard, Man Ray, Winston Churchill, Christian Dior, Catherine Deneuve, Edith Piaf and Jacques Brel and many others have all fallen in love with this incredible village, one of the prettiest on the French Riviera… and also one of the most visited.

Of note: the Church of Saint-Jacques-le-Majeur, the chapel of Saint-Barthélemy, the car museum and the photography museum.

Ramatuelle. It is impossible not to covet the houses here. Wouldn't you love to live here, or there, or perhaps on the square...?

RAMATUELLE

Saint-Tropez with its famous Pampelonne beach is just 10 kilometres away, and closer still, just a stone's throw away, lie beautiful coves with their exceptional sea floor and miles of golden sand stretching below the village, squeezed tightly within its ramparts. Built on the hillside in the heart of the peninsula, Ramatuelle has a particularly active cultural scene with its jazz, classical music and theatre festivals. Many celebrities have fallen in love with this place and stayed there.

Of note: the Porte Sarrasine, the bakers' ovens, the lords' house, the old cemetery, the Camarat lighthouse and the coastal footpath.

FRENCH RIVIERA

*Gassin, with Grimaud below.
The choice is yours.
One is charming, the other
delightful. Which one will
you fall in love with?*

GASSIN

Gassin is located in the middle of the Saint-Tropez peninsula, perched on a rocky promontory just 4 kilometres from the sea. The village has kept its winding streets and old picturesque houses. Its geographical location is rather exceptional. It overlooks a landscape of vineyards, wooded areas and the Gulf of Saint-Tropez! There is a magnificent view from the ramparts over to the Iles d'Or, up to the snowy summits of the Alps, and over the Massif des Maures.

On the sea front, Port-Gassin is a newcomer to the coast, an extension of the existing lake complexes of Port-Grimaud and the Marines de Cogolin. The Templars have also left their mark there.

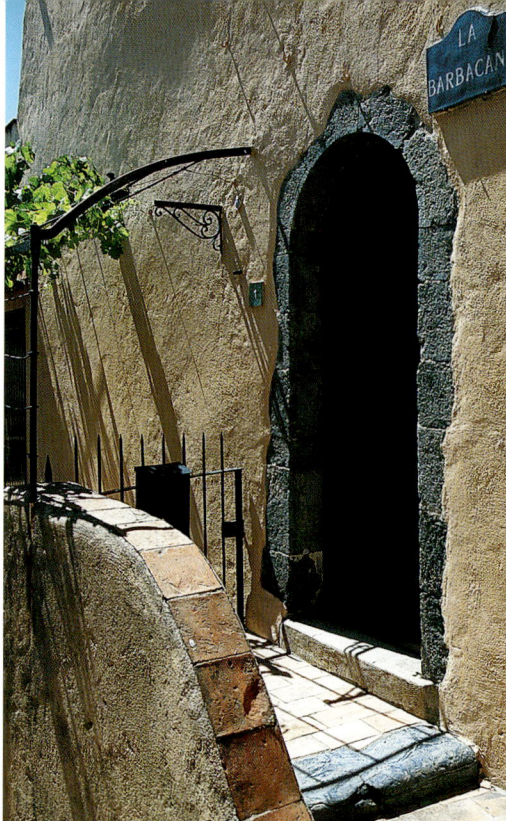

Visit the historic remains: the ramparts, the church, the presbytery and the Chapel of Notre-Dame-de-la-Compassion.

GRIMAUD

Surrounded by the Maures mountains and standing on the edge of the Gulf of Saint-Tropez, Grimaud has managed to preserve its medieval character. The village is charming, with cobbled, flower-bedecked winding imaginatively from the Romanesque church to the ruins of the feudal castle. Walking around the village, you will come across some magnificent old houses that have been superbly renovated. The village is perched on the hillside in a most beautiful setting. Just a few kilometres further along the coast lies the lakeside complex of Port-Grimaud, designed by the architect François Spoerry. The canals of Port-Grimaud are internationally renowned and draw thousands of visitors each year.

Of note: ruins of the feudal castle, the church of Saint-Michel (11th century), the Bridge of Fairies, the Chapel of Saint-Roch.

Port-Grimaud.

The windmill above Grimaud.

Bormes-les-Mimosas, one of the finest of France's "villages in bloom".

BORMES-LES-MIMOSAS

Protected by the Maures mountains, nestling in greenery, the old village of Bormes is set back from the sea and the port. It is listed as one of the finest of France's "villages in bloom".

This attractive, medieval village is often compared to traditional Provençal nativity scenes, with its sloping streets carving their way through vaulted alleyways, *cuberts*, staircases, old houses with pink tiled roofs and flowers on the balconies.

Of note: the ruins of the castle overlooking the village, the Rue Rompi-Cuou with its 83 steps leading to the Place du Bazar, home to the old trunk of an elm tree planted after the 2nd Republic of 1848 as a symbol of

One of the steeples in Bormes.

liberty, the chapel of Saint-François, and the chapel of Notre-Dame-de-Constance at 324 metres above sea level with its orientation table diagram and superb panoramic view of the sea, the islands and the Massif des Maures.

On a small peninsula in the hamlet of Cabasson, an old fishing village, lies the famous fort of Bregançon, the summer residence of the Presidents of the French Republic.

Collobrières

Set far away from the crowded coastlines, this unique village is a cluster of houses gathered around the 19th century ivy-covered Gothic church of Saint-Pons.
In the very heart of the Maures forest, of which it is the capital, Collobrières is famous for its chestnut groves and cork oaks. It is a peaceful village with a whole string of cafes and terraces by the river Real Collobrier that runs through the village. The picturesque old houses resemble a backdrop for a play and when evening falls, the village elders sit and chat on the old 12th century humpback bridge. The charming and shady Place de la Mairie has a very beautiful old fountain. Collobrières is the ideal starting point for a walk through the Maures mountains, with a dozen roads, tracks and footpaths running around the village and heading into the national forests of La Londe-les-Maures, Pierrefeu, Pignans and Mayons.
Of note: the old medieval village, the ruins of the church of Saint-Pons (12th century), the Carthusian monastery of La Verne (12 kilometres away) and the standing stones on the Plateau Lambert.

Up in the hills behind the Riviera, the pace, rhythm and scent of life are very different.

The Carthusian monastery of La Verne

"I approach the abbey and discover all the old buildings, the oldest of which date from the 12th century, and the most recent of which are inhabited by shepherds.

Nowhere else in the world have I felt in my heart such a weight of melancholy as in this ancient, sinister monastery [...] Behind the abbey, a mountain stretches up to heaven; a chestnut grove surrounds the ruins, and in front lies a valley; in the distance are more valleys. Pine trees, pine trees, an ocean of pine trees and on the summits on the horizon, more pine trees.

And then I left." (Guy de Maupassant, "Sur l'eau de Saint-Tropez à Monte-Carlo).

Perhaps Maupassant was in a rather sombre mood that day, or perhaps the imposing buildings of this Carthusian monastery were too darkly shaded by the valley.

Whatever the reason, it is a pity, since this abbey, founded in 1170 by Pierre Isnard, Bishop of Toulon, is a marvel.

It is definitely not a happy place, but then again, after three fires and such a turbulent history as this place, what monument would be?

The road to the abbey is sublime, winding next to a stream through hundred-year-old trees. The last stretch is a dirt road, so drivers take it easy!

The little village squares are filled with the shady scent of plane trees.

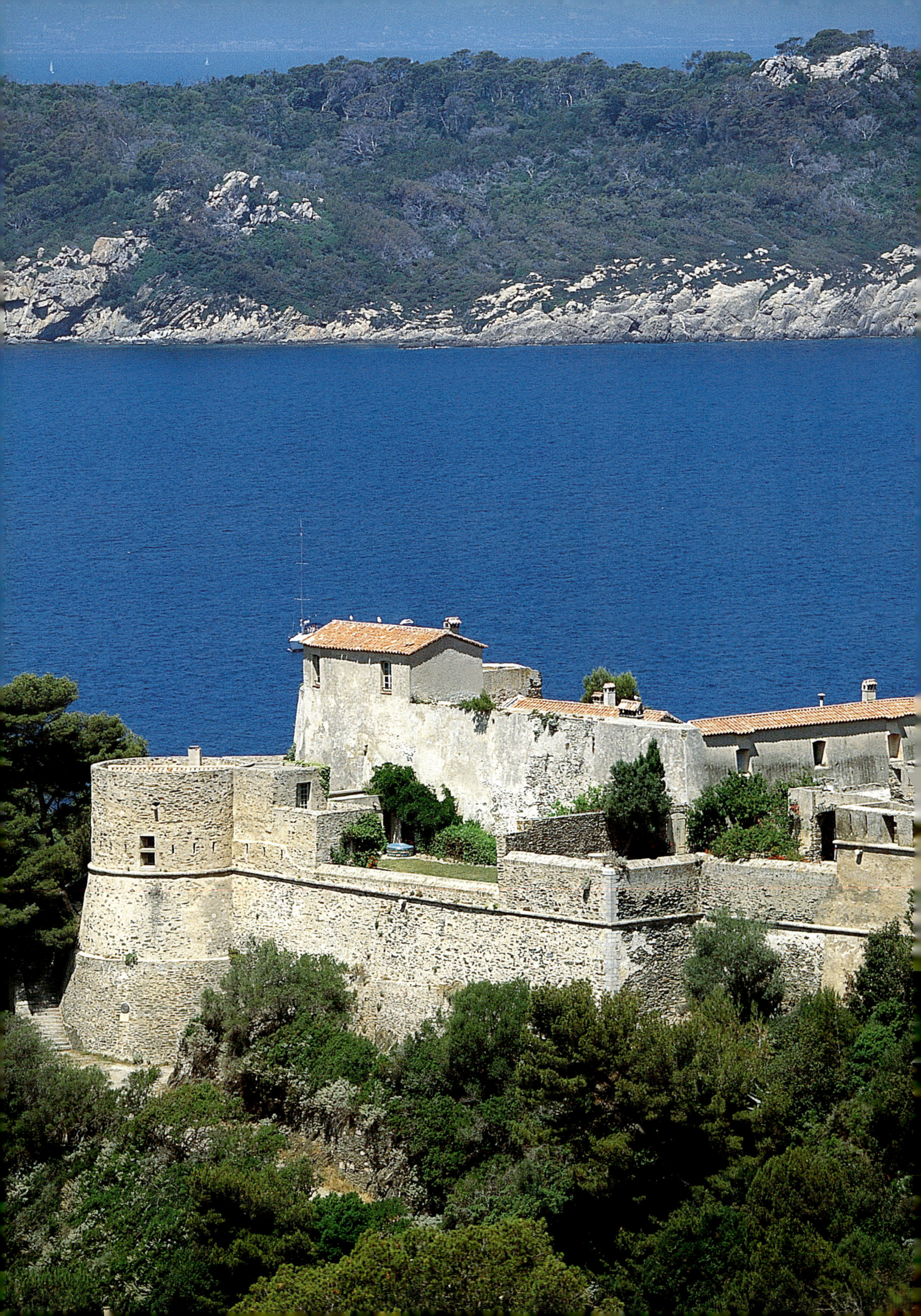

The Islands

ILES DE LERINS
Sainte-Marguerite
Saint-Honorat
ILES D'HYÈRES
Porquerolles
Ports-Cros
Iles du Levant

"Today I finally got an idea of what the Mediterranean can be like. I was stunned. The pale blue horizon, lavender and violet blue. The islands near Cannes were purple - at midday! blues and greens like shining opals. [...] Wonderful for painters. The clearest atmosphere you could possibly imagine. Almost like in the desert."
(Henry Miller in a letter to Anaïs Nin)

ILES DE LERINS

The Iles de Lérins were first occupied by the Ligurians for a long period and have retained some important archaeological remains. Sainte-Marguerite then became a point of call for the Romans, along the shipping route to Spain. Both of the islands have been pillaged throughout the centuries.

The island of Saint-Honorat has its own unique destiny. Saint Honorat himself founded a monastery here in around 400 AD, later to become part of the Benedictine order.

Sainte-Marguerite was a dependency of the monastery until 1633, when, under Richelieu, it became royal territory because of its very important strategic position. It was under Spanish rule for two years, during which time the Spanish began work on the fortification of the island. The fort was then completed by Vauban and later became a state prison, home to some famous prisoners to say the least. There was the Man in the Iron Mask of course, as well as Marshal Bazaine, whose escape from here is definitely a case of fact stranger than fiction. Other prisoners included Mamelukes and Huguenots.

Left:
Porquerolles.

"As we approached the island of Saint-Honorat, we passed over a bare red rock, bristling like a porcupine. It was so rough, armed with teeth, spikes and claws, that one could hardly walk on it. You have to step in the hollows between its armour, and move forward cautiously. It is called Saint-Ferréol. Some earth, who knows from where, has built up in the holes and cracks in the rock, and in there a type of lily and charming blue irises have grown, as if their seeds had fallen from the sky. It was on this strange rock in the middle of the sea that Paganini's body was buried and hidden for five years.

Such an adventure is worthy of this brilliant, macabre artist who was said to be possessed by the devil, with his strange appearance, body and face, his superhuman talent and acute thinness, all of which made him into a legendary being, like one of Hoffmann's characters. As he was returning to his home city of Genoa in the company of his son who was the only one who could understand him since his voice had become so weak, he died of cholera in Nice on May 27, 1840. So his son took his father's body and sailed for Italy, but the Genoese clergy refused to give this demonic character a resting place. The Court of Rome was consulted but did not dare to give its authorisation. Nevertheless, the body was about to be disembarked when the city council intervened, refusing disembarkation since the artist had died of cholera. At that time, Genoa was already devastated by this disease, but the argument was put forward that the presence of this new corpse could make the scourge worse. So Paganini's son returned to Marseilles, where he was refused entrance to the port for the same reasons. Then, he headed for Cannes where again he was refused access. And so he stayed at sea, the waves rocking the dead body of this great, bizarre artist rejected by men everywhere he went. He did not know what to do, where to go, where to take this body that was so sacred for him, when he saw the bare rock of Saint-Ferréol rising out of the sea. He landed there with the coffin, which he had buried in the middle of the island. Only in 1845 did he return with two friends to recover his father's remains and take them to Genoa. Wouldn't we have perhaps preferred this extraordinary violinist to have stayed on this sharp rocky island, where the waves sing in the strange cracks in the rock?" (Guy de Maupassant, "Sur l'eau de Saint-Tropez à Monte-Carlo").

You can get to the Iles de Lérins by boat from Cannes, Golfe-Juan and Juan-les-Pins. Information: Compagnie Maritime Cannoise, Promenade Pantiéro, in Cannes next to the Palais des Festivals.

SAINTE-MARGUERITE : A DELIGHTFUL ISLAND

This is the larger of the two islands, 3 kilometres long by about 900 metres wide. There are no cars, no noise other than the lapping of the waves, the wind in the sails and in the Aleppo pine trees, and the song of cicadas for six months of the year. This island is truly paradise, with its luxuriant beauty, luscious plants and flowers, eucalyptus, maritime pines, an abundance of turquoise water and calm coves nestling in rocks smoothed by the tides.

Legend has it that the island was named after one of Saint Honorat's sisters, who was the head of a community of nuns. At the time, women were not allowed on the island of Saint Honorat. The legend holds that Marguerite's brother, having withdrawn from the world, told her that he could only see here once a year, when the almond trees blossomed, but that his determination melted when a miracle occurred: Marguerite planted an almond tree that blossomed every month.

In reality, it would seem that the island got its name from the chapel dedicated to Marguerite d'Antioche.

Recently, the remains of the small Roman city of Léro were discovered here, with the remains a few houses, some frescoes, vases and household objects, enough evidence of the Roman art of living... Unfortunately the remains cannot be visited.

You can however visit the Musée de la Mer, in the fortified castle whose construction that Richelieu ordered to be built and which was finished by Vauban. There are ceramics and glass works, amphora from Roman and Saracen ships, as well as some objects from the Léro excavation.

But the most enchanting attraction for visitors throughout the ages is the story (part myth, part legend) of the enigmatic "Man in the Iron Mask". One of the theories is that he was the illegitimate brother of Louis XIV, but there are many different versions, each one stranger than the next.

A few months after the death of the minister, Mazarin, a quite unprecedented event took place, and a great deal of ink has been spilled over the identity of the mysterious character.

Sainte-Marguerite. The island is named after Saint Marguerite of Antioche.

The Man in the Iron Mask

Initially incarcerated in the Pignerol fortress in Piedmont, he stayed in the Ile Sainte-Marguerite prison for eleven years, from 1687 to 1698. He died in the Bastille in 1703 after thirty-seven years of imprisonment. In the 18th century, a few lines by Voltaire in "Le Siècle de Louis XIV" generated interest and curiosity over the mystery and identity of the prisoner, which historians, novelists and readers maintain passionately to this day. Who was behind the iron mask? Louis XIV's twin brother, Molière, Count Mattioli, the Duke of Guise, a woman, Nabo the Negro, a Dominican monk, Blaise Pascal…?
It is said that the prisoner fell in love whilst in prison and that he had a son, given "in good part" ("di buona parte" in Italian), to some trustworthy people, and that this child was named Bonaparte. According to one of the many legends, he was the Emperor's grandfather.
More than sixty different possible names have been put forward for this "prisoner whose name no-one knows, whose face no-one has seen, a living mystery, a shadow, an enigma, a problem" (Victor Hugo). Three centuries later, the enigma remains, much to the delight of mystery lovers and seekers of legends, like a black hole in history.

Voltaire wrote these lines in his work "Le Siècle de Louis XIV".

"In the greatest secret, was sent to the castle on the island of Sainte-Marguerite in the Sea of Provence, an unknown prisoner, taller than average, young and with the most handsome and noble face…"

SAINT-HONORAT: THE HOUSE OF GOD

1500 metres long and 400 metres wide, it is separated from Sainte-Marguerite by the channel known as the Plateau de Milieu, which in summer you can practically walk across because there are so many boats.

As on Sainte-Marguerite, the flora here is enchanting: Italian stone pines and maritime pines fill the air with

THE ISLANDS

The blue waters between Saint-Honorat and Sainte-Marguerite.

their resinous scent that brings back memories of happy holidays.

Like many other small islands along the Mediterranean coast, the smaller of the two Lérins islands off Cannes is home to a monastery. The monks grew vines, lavender, and orange trees, and made honey and liqueurs from aromatic plants.

Saint-Honorat, along with Saint Caprais and some other companions, arrived on the island between 400 and 410. He settled on one of the two islands, "Lérina". With the blessing of Léonce, Bishop of Fréjus, he founded a community which in 427 became a "huge monastery". Pilgrims came in hoards because a visit to the island earned them as many indulgences as a trip to the Holy Land. They would walk barefoot around the island, and a pope even came to do penance there.

Saint-Honorat.

Visiting the island

The island of Saint-Honorat is owned by the Cistercian Congregation of the Immaculate Conception and is open to visitors all year round. Due to its long monastic history and its two beautiful buildings, the island has a unique atmosphere steeped in peace and tradition. The natural surroundings, tamed and cultivated by the monks over the ages through the planting of vines and olive trees, add to this atmosphere of serenity and meditation. You can walk around the island and visit some of the buildings. The fortified monastery stands on the south side of the island, surrounded by the sea on three sides. Originally a keep first built in the 11th century, little by little it was expanded and transformed to become a fortified monastery that was home to both a community of monks and a garrison of soldiers in the 15th century. The Chapel of La Trinité stands on the eastern tip of the island.

The present monastery is in the centre of the island and is home to a Cistercian community of thirty monks living in work and prayer. The church is always open for prayer, and you may also participate in a service with the monks. The rest of the monastery is not open to visitors.

Services: mass, 11.25 a.m. on weekdays, 9.50 am on Sundays and public holidays. Other services are at 12.25 pm, and 2.15 pm in Winter and 2.30 pm in Summer.

The Saint-Honorat monastery (photo H. Champollion).

Nectar of paradise

The little known "vigne du Seigneur" (vine of the Lord), half-hidden behind the pine and olive trees and lavender fields, dates from the Middle Ages. For the last six years, the monks have called upon the wine making skills of an oenologist from Les Arcs, and have begun cultivating this little stretch of God's land, under the supervision of Abbot Dom Nicolas Aubertin, a member of the order of Cîteaux.

One and a half hectares of vines give a light, floral white wine (ugni blanc and clairette). 2 more hectares are given over to a red wine, a syrah yet to be produced, whilst the Vendange des Moines (approximately 8000 bottles per year) covers nearly 7 hectares! These wines can be found on some of the best tables of the French Riviera and even in Japan. As for the historic Lérina liqueur, this is part of a monastic tradition dating back to the last century when the brand was first registered. The latest changes to the formula were made by a monk about fifty years ago. A careful choice of plants, precise proportions and closely supervised distillation give a unique liqueur with beautiful amber colours, full of the island's subtle scents.

(Photo P. Thebault)

THE ISLANDS

In 660, Saint Aygulphe instated Benedictine rules. Aygulphe, who died in so doing, has always been considered a martyr.

The monastery's influence was widespread. Saint Patrick left from here to evangelise Ireland; Saint Hilaire, Bishop of Arles, came from here, as did Saint Loup, who stopped Attila; as well as Saint Cassien, Saint Cézaire and Saint Salvien.

Around 732, Saint Porcaire and his five hundred and fifty monks were massacred by the Saracens.

Subsequently, the political importance of Saint Honorat was such that the entire coastline, from Antibes to the Esterel, including Vallauris, Le Cannet, Mougins and Valbonne depended upon it, and Rome encouraged its development in order to reinstate its authority in the region. The monastery was confiscated and closed during the French Revolution, and it was not until 1859 that the Abbot of Sénanque re-established Cistercian life, rules which are still followed by the monks there today.

Ora et labora (Photo P. Thebault)

FRENCH RIVIERA

Some species of flora and fauna, very common until a few years ago, are now rapidly disappearing from the island's sea floor.
Unfortunately, few people take much interest in the destruction of spondylus, mother of pearl and other seashells. The "arca", a type of red mussel, used to cover the rocks at La Fourmigue, and the "arapèdes" (limpets) used to be the delight of fishermen. Today there are practically none to be found. However, a few specimens of pteria hirundo, a seashell named after its swallow-like shape, can still be found in these waters.
Living in small colonies but different from its cousin the oyster, which is mainly found in rocks, this seashell is found on gorgonian coral.

Underwater cliffs with red gorgonian coral (photo E. Dutrieux).

Red coral (photo E. Dutrieux).

Starfish can be found in the most fabulous shapes at depths of more than 50 metres. As for the spondylus, "the hinged oyster" (named after its shape), this was one of the most common shellfish of our coasts until about twenty years ago.
Colonies of the "crayon" sea urchin were also frequently found here on sandy seafloors below 20 meters, but today there are only a few specimens and only in very deep waters.

Just a slight increase in water temperature is enough to kill gorgonians, sponges and corals. Some species are disappearing, others are colonising the coastline.
Age-old marine "fossils" like the coelacanth (400 million years), perhaps the first link in the chain of terrestrial vertebrates, or the nautilus, a cephalopod (like octopus and squid), the last survivor of a family of molluscs that lived in the seas during the Palaeozoic period (end of the primary era). The nautilus mainly feeds on dead prey, which it identifies thanks to its highly developed chemical sensitivity. Fossilised specimens, commonly called "ammonites", are easily found.

The islands' shipwrecks

Although often invisible, ancient shipwrecks scatter the sea floor from the Cap d'Antibes to the Iles de Lérins. At times just a small clue gives them away: an octopus nest or gorgonian on the sea floor for example. Presently, seventeen ancient shipwrecks have been counted between the Grande Grenille (to the east of the Cap d'Antibes) and the Iles de Lérins: three Greek or Etruscan ships and fourteen Roman ships. Were the Romans really such bad sailors?

There are four of five centuries between the Greek and Roman shipwrecks, but the sailing conditions would have been identical. The ships were built along the same lines, without a rudder at the sternpost and with practically no keel, and the rigging was practically identical. They had no maps or compasses, relying on sailors who already knew the area to guide them around the rocks. But for the Romans, the profit motive was so strong that they tended to unreasonably overload their ships with the inevitable results.

The cloister at Saint Honorat. (photo H. Champollion)

Saint Benoît and the Cistercians

From the very beginnings of monastic life, monastic rules were designed to support and guide those learning to live an evangelical life, or what the ancients called an apostolic life, that is a life that imitates that of Christ's apostles. This is the case, for example, of the first rules of Lérins, called the "Rules of the Fathers" written by Saint Honorat in around 410 AD.

Cistercian monks have been living on this island since 1869, continuing to interpret these rules and living together in a fraternal community, according to the Gospel. There are a certain number of key words to describe their spirituality, such as Desert, Stability, Inner Peace, Work, Fraternal Community, School of Charity... all of which express both the Gospel itself and monastic concepts, so that the monks may continue to live today much as Honorat did in the 5th century.

FRENCH RIVIERA

ILES D'HYÈRES, THE GOLDEN ISLANDS

It was Frederic Mistral himself who christened these islands the "Iles d'Or" or "golden islands". Just one look at the rocks sparkling like melting gold above the sea, or lighting up in the still evening air, is enough to illustrate the full meaning of this simple and perfect name.

The shortest route to the islands is from the Tour Fondue at the very end of the Giens peninsula. There are also boats from the port of Bormes and the port of Le Lavandou.

Map labels

- D 559
- Bormes-les-Mimosas
- Rayol-Canadel-sur-Mer
- Cap Nègre
- CORNICHE DES MAURES
- CAVALAIRE
- La Londe-les-Maures
- Le Lavandou
- Salins
- D 42
- Les Salins d'Hyères
- Port de Miramar
- Cap de Léoube
- 186 ▲ Cabasson
- Port de Bormes
- Le Gau
- Ayguade-Plage
- TOULON/HYÈRES LE PALYESTRE
- D 97
- Cap de Brégançon
- Cap Bénat
- ST-TROPEZ
- Salins
- RADE D'HYÈRES
- Presqu'Île de Giens
- Pointe de la Calle Rousse
- Phare du Titan
- D 97
- Giens
- Cap de l'Esterel
- Îles d'Hyères
- Pointe du Castellas
- Île du Grand Ribaud
- Cap des Mèdes
- Anc. Batterie
- Grande Passe
- Île de Bagaud
- Fort du Moulin
- Fort de l'Estissac
- Fort de l'Éminence
- Le Grand-Avis
- Pointe de l'Arête
- Les Pierres Blanches
- Île du Levant
- Batterie Bon-Renaud
- Fort de l'Alycatre
- Anc. Batterie
- Fort de la Repentance
- Pointe de Port-Man
- TOULON
- Île du Petit Langoustier
- Fort Ste-Agathe
- Anc. Batterie
- Port-Cros
- Port-Man
- Héliopolis
- Le Grand Cap
- Fort du Grand Langoustier
- Porquerolles
- Fortin de la Vigie
- Pointe Maupertuis
- Île de Porquerolles
- Vallon de la Solitude
- Île de Port-Cros
- Cap d'Arme
- Phare et Calanques de l'Oustaou-de-Diou
- PARC DE PORT-CROS

0 — 5 km

THE ISLAND OF PORQUEROLLES

Ulysses, who is said to have landed on Porquerolles during his legendary voyage, would not be surprised today were he to land in this tiny port with its secluded jetty, a rocky point covered with maritime pines, a few white and pink houses hidden among the palm trees, mimosas and tamarisk.

This is where Jean-Paul Belmondo and Anna Karina's journey ends in "Pierrot le Fou", this is where children are conceived even when all hope has been lost (the writer Martin du Gard), here that novels are started that change the course of history - Sartre's "Les Mouches"...

The first view of Porquerolles when arriving by ferry.

Right: **Swimming at Porquerolles is always worth it.**

"An island that stretches out then shrinks progressively at each of its pointed ends, giving Porquerolles the air of a crescent moon."

This is how one discovers Porquerolles, when you disembark from the island ferry that also goes to Port-Cros and the Levant... Scrubland with rockroses burnt by the sun, eucalyptus trees, the song of cicadas, seagulls fighting against the wind above the sharp rocks, the surf and splash of the waves churned up by the Mistral wind. Porquerolles is a model of insularity, an island balancing between land and sea. It stretches harmoniously around the central village, clear in the summer under its palm trees and stone pines, misty in the winter surrounded by

T H E I S L A N D S

carefully ploughed fields. For any traveller approaching the island, the effect is immediate. The large square with its eucalyptus trees, the small church, the fishermen's houses...and carts to transport your luggage since there are no cars here. The village shares its name with the whole of the island. Nestling in a miniature bay with the large beach

FRENCH RIVIERA

of La Courtade at the north end, it is home to a small port for the pleasure boats and motor launches that link the island to the mainland. The village was built one hundred and fifty years ago beneath the 15th century fort of Sainte-Agathe, to provide shelter for the families of soldiers in the garrison. For many years, the island served as a military camp for convalescent soldiers. The injured from the Crimean war and the campaign in Madagascar were sent here for treatment.

The Stations of the Cross at the Church of Sainte-Anne are fascinating, with fourteen huge carved walnut panels, the work of a soldier of the African battalion who stayed on the island in 1868. Other more or less ruined forts bear witness to the long military presence here. The oldest is the fort of l'Alicastre, built under Richelieu and named, so legend has it, after a fabulous monster (the Lycastre) slain by a mysterious knight. It was used as a prison from 1848 to 1852 - this seems to be the second calling for many of these buildings - and, of course, tradition has it that the Man in the Iron Mask was locked up here when the ship bringing him to the Ile Sainte-Marguerite was forced to land at Porquerolles due to contrary winds.

Although it is not a national park, Porquerolles is protected today and no more roads will be built. As in the rest of the islands, cars are prohibited, and one walks or cycles to the

Porquerolles in the foreground, with Port-Cros in the backgro

THE ISLANDS

FRENCH RIVIERA

Fine cuisine

Porquerolles loves good cooking. For example, to add taste to a white sea bream cooked on a wood fire, the fish is smeared with sea urchin coral. This is served with a salad of "coustellines", a sort of dandelion with thick, sweet leaves, which grows by the sea and thus has a slightly salty taste.
In winter, you can sample fresh kumquat and arbutus berry jam.
In the spring, the thin sweet-smelling stems of young wild asparagus can be gathered to season omelettes or rice.

Right: **Port-Cros, where nature conservation and an idyllic setting go hand in hand.**

beaches. A typical tour of the island leads to the lighthouse (96 metres) on the southern end and then crosses the whole width of the island. From the summit one discovers a beautiful view of most of the island, the Langoustier hills, the fort of Sainte-Agathe, the semaphore and, in the distance, the Maures mountains and their ochre cliffs plunging into the sea. There is no road going right around Porquerolles. Cunningly concealed footpaths lead to wild coves on the south side or sandy beaches on the north and west side, and to the rocky points of the Cap des Medès, the Grand-Langoustier or l'Alicastre. The footpaths to the view point are somewhat more demanding, but worth the effort for the view of the coast or of the island itself, a vast, calm and practically deserted expanse of beautiful Aleppo pine forests, cork, lentisks, arbutus trees, a few sturdy vines, and cicadas singing in the sweet-smelling maquis, with here and there, orange, lemon and mandarin orchards. The surrounding seafloor is also of interest (sponge, coral etc) and much appreciated by divers.

"I am telling you of a shore where the mythological traces of the Mediterranean produce an admirable mixture of laziness and hard work". (Jean Cocteau)

Winemaking on the island

Domaine de l'Ile 1998

There are two private estates that are currently expanding their vineyards: the Domaine de l'Ile and the Domaine de La Courtade. The first, about thirty hectares, is run by Sébastien Le Ber, grandson of M. Fournier, and who has taken over from his parents in the family tradition.
The reputation of his rosé, the first to obtain the "appellation contrôlée" (AOC Provence) is now firmly established. The secret of this success lies in hand picking and the assembly of five grapes: Cinsault, Carignan, Tibouren, Grenache and Mourvèdre. Nearly the entire production (450 hectolitres) is sold on site. Meanwhile, Mr. Vidal, who has bought the Domaine de la Courtade, has been renovating about thirty hectares of the vineyard since 1983. His ambition is to create an attractive vineyard of good quality and low yield (maximum 45 hectolitres) and ultimately create an "appellation Porquerolles".
He also wishes to produce a red wine, based mainly on Mourvèdre, a very difficult grape to grow.
White and red wines are aged in new and old oak barrels using traditional methods.
Some of these elegant conical bottles, known as "bordelaise tradition", end up in the hands of overseas enthusiasts. Others are undergoing strange experiments: presently stored underwater at 20 meters below sea level, they will be tested in about ten years time.

Domaine de la Courtade

Domaine de la Courtade

PORT-CROS, TREASURE ISLAND

On this green island with its twelve springs (two of which contain iron), the maquis can at times be impenetrable, a tangle of lentisks, Estrella gold and arbutus trees.

The charm and simplicity of its way of life turns entirely around its luxuriant, untamed landscape. The protected area for fauna and flora extends 600 metres from the coast and includes the small islands of Rascas, La Gabinière, Bagaud and various neighbouring islets. Fishing and underwater hunting are prohibited, and sailing speeds are strictly controlled.

Since ancient times, the history of Port-Cros, known to Greek sailors as the Mesé or middle island, has been inextricably linked to that of Porquerolles. Smaller than Porquerolles (640 hectares, 4.5 km long and 2 km wide), its present name, "the hollow port" is due to the deep indentation of its harbour.

FRENCH RIVIERA

Port-Cros has been a national park since 1963 and has become a veritable refuge for fauna.

Like the islands here, Port-Cros was first populated by Ligurians and then by the Lérins monks who came to clear it in the 5th century. In the Middle Ages, it suffered a monotonous succession of invasions and was pillaged by pirates for five centuries. A former property of the Count of Beauregard, who leased the hunting grounds there, it became a national park in 1963. Inside the island, camping and hunting are prohibited and plants may not be removed. It was in this idyllic setting that Melchior de Vogüe set his novel "Jean d'Agrève" (1897), a work of some notoriety at the start of the century. Today you can still visit the heroine, Helen's, manor at the entrance to the Valley of Solitude. Another pleasant way to explore the island's wonderful vegetation is to head for the bay of Port-Man, a remarkable semi-circle of greenery. Access is via a rather steep but shady path winding through beautiful scenery across the entire length of the island. From the Col de Port-Man, there is a view of the Ile du Levant, directly in front of the island, and the Maures mountains in the distance. From the bay, sheltered from the northern winds, you can walk on to the picturesque hamlet of Port-Cros via small footpaths leading to the Pointe de la Galère, crossing the Vallon du Janet, the Plateau de la

FRENCH RIVIERA

The island's bright cliffs.

Marma and along the La Palu beach and the Vallon Noir. There are many walking opportunities even for solitary walkers, particularly off-season. Don't miss the magnificent view of the sharp cliffs along the southern coast of the island.

Underwater life is full of unlikely shapes and colours: a moray eel (left) and a grouper (above).
(Photos E. Dutrieux.)

Protected beauty

Certain plants found on Port-Cros are unique, such as the Teucrium marum *or even some of the mushrooms that thrive in the Mediterranean undergrowth, such as the* lactarius sanguiflus *and* armillaria. *The fauna lives in total freedom and some rare species can be found there, since this vast protected area is unique in the Mediterranean. Herring gulls, shags, Cory's shearwaters, as well as peregrine falcons, sparrowhawks, bluebirds, bee-eaters and hoopoes. Other species regularly stop over here on their annual migration routes: sparrows, wood pigeons, turtle doves and pink flamingos. The surrounding marine life is as intense and precious, particularly on the southern coast where the water is extremely pure and gives a clear view of the sea floor at more than 40 metres. Plants, moss and algae (samphire, lavatera, statice, euphorbia and the rare silver teucrium) cover the rocks. Here and along the east coast are the ideal spots for scuba diving (which is authorised) and inside caves you can come across grouper, dentis and moray eels, brush up against white sea bream with their slanting stripes, rouquiers, mullet and other fish in all shapes and colours that live freely in these protected waters.*

F R E N C H   R I V I E R A

"Mum, is it true that boats can breathe?"

Right: *A blue world of wood, water, wind and silence.*

THE ILE DU LEVANT, THE ISLAND OF BIRDS

This is the island of butterflies (more than 60 species), dragonflies and birds.

In fact it is the perfect island for all winged species - a long and narrow rocky ridge, not more than 1 km at its widest, 8 km long, rising to about 100 metres above sea level above sharp rocks. Here you can find garnet, black tourmaline, staurolites, and the highly sought after *pierre de fer*, a real find for amateur geologists. The flora is less abundant than in the neighbouring islands of Port-Cros and Porquerolles, but you can find one rare botanical specimen, apple grass *(Teucrium massiliense)*, named after its characteristic scent. A refuge for Anchorites in the early days of Christianity, today it is a paradise for naturists, and welcomes an ever increasing number of nudism enthusiasts, quite astonishing for an island that for centuries provided shelter to a variety of religious orders. The Lérins monks built an outpost of their abbey there; the Benedictines, then from the 15th century the Brothers of the Cross resided there, in a monastery, the remains of which can still be seen today in the Vallon du Jas Vieux.

It was in 1931 that the Ile du Levant's destiny changed course when the Doctors Gaston and André Durville began building the first naturist resort in France and called it Héliopolis.

The Ile du Levant at that time had no more than about fifteen inhabitants.

Things have changed since then, as more and more naturists come for a taste of this idyllic lifestyle, although they do share the island with the French army, which has fenced off a large part of the island for military manoeuvres. All this and more, on the purest of islands with its marvellous, austere beauty and waters so clear that you can see entire shoals of fish wriggling joyfully by.

119

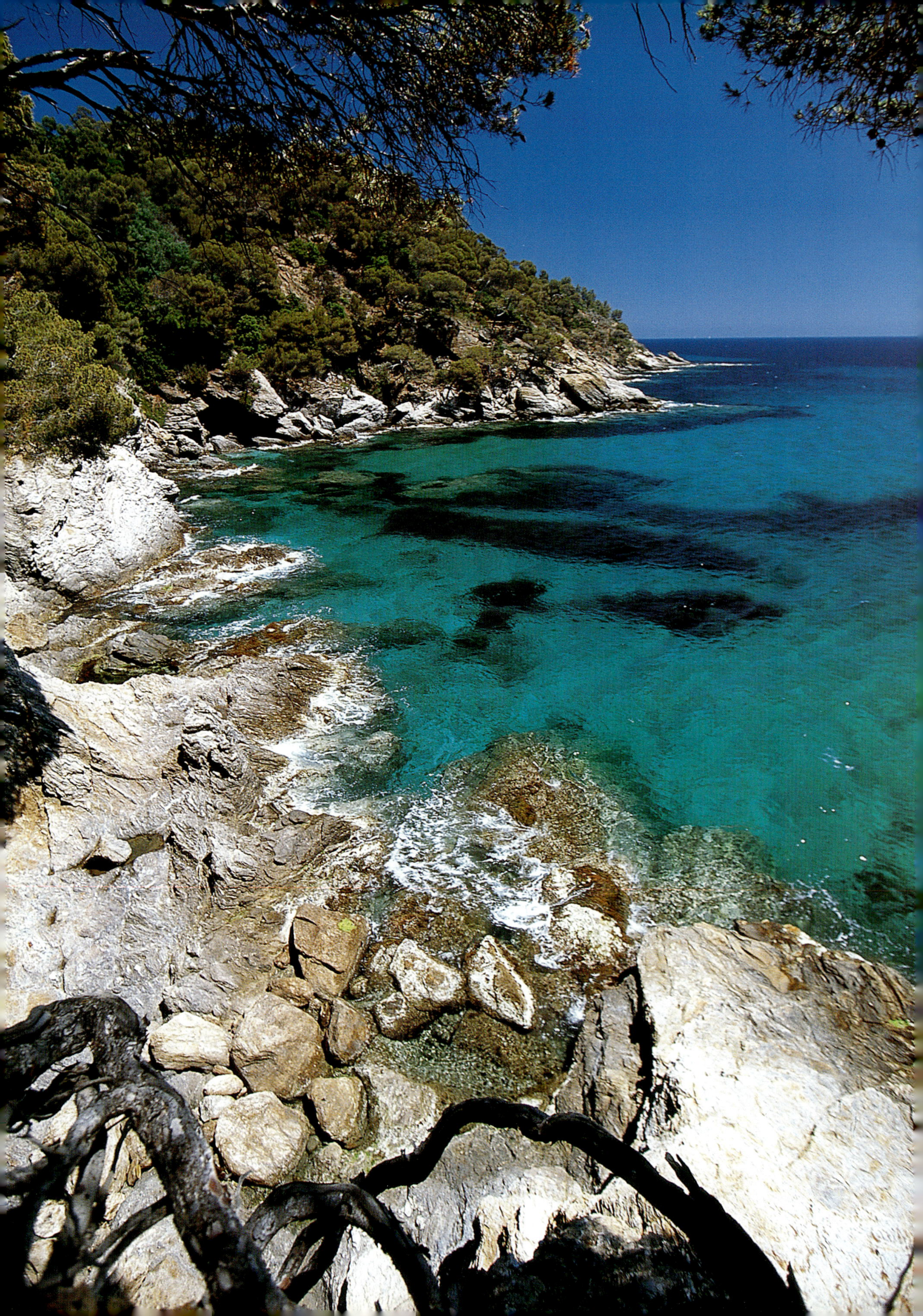

BIBLIOGRAPHY

Guide books
Splendeurs des jardins de la Côte d'Azur, L. Jones, Flammarion
Les fruits de mon moulin, Roger Vergé, Flammarion
Guide du naturaliste dans le Midi de la France, Delachaux et Niestlé
Grasse, la cité aromatique, Serre
Guide Côte d'Azur, vacances secrètes, Arthaud
La Côte d'Azur des écrivains, Edisud
Côte d'Azur, principauté de Monaco, Michelin
Provence - Côte d'Azur, Hachette, les Guides Bleus

Literature
Sur l'eau de Saint-Tropez à Monte-Carlo, Guy de Maupassant
Belle du Seigneur, Albert Cohen
The Razor's Edge, Somerset Maugham
Marée basse, Cyril Connolly
Tendre comme le souvenir, Guillaume Apollinaire
Tender is the Night, Francis Scott Fitzgerald
Journal, André Gide
Œuvres complètes, Blaise Cendrars
Le Testament d'Orphée, Jean Cocteau
Complete works of Blaise Cendrars
L'Entrave, La vagabonde, Colette
Gilles, Pierre Drieu La Rochelle
Save me the Waltz, Zelda Fitzgerald
Le Frère de la Côte, Joseph Conrad
L'intelligence des fleurs, Maurice Maeterlinck
Voyage de noces, Patrick Modiano
Diaries of Katherine Mansfield
Diaries of Anaïs Nin
Vingt-quatre heures dans la vie d'une femme, Stefan Zweig
Bains de mer – Méditerranée, mer des surprises, Paul Morand
Autres rivages, Vladimir Nabokov
Simenon, Pierre Assouline

A hot, sunny afternoon at the Serre de la Madone. The cat meows as an angry arrow dives towards him, attacking relentlessly from above. Trying to keep up appearances, the cat pretends to wash itself, ears pricked up, acting sly in the face of this black screeching. The blackbird refuses to give up, aiming for the eyes. A nearby fountain murmurs indifferently.

Left: **The splendid Rayol estate.**

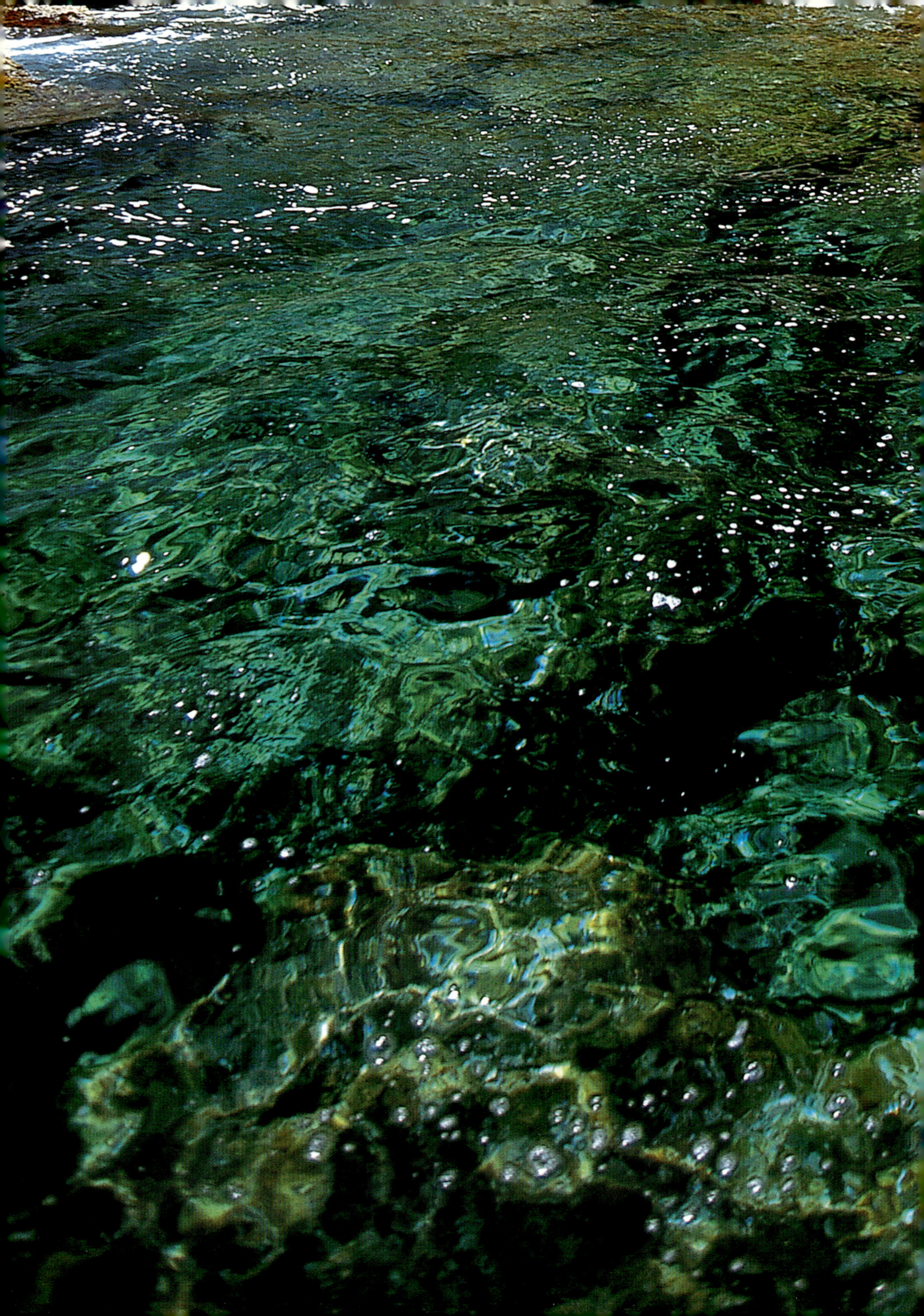

Recommended addresses

For olive oil:

The oil mills in the Levens area near Nice in the Alpes-Maritimes: the Saint-Blaise oil mill and museum, the abbey of Notre-Dame-de-la-Paix at Castagniers, the castle and museum at Tourette-sur-Levens etc.

Some olive oil mills on the French Riviera: Auribeau-sur-Siagne - RD9 - moulin de Sault; Moulin Sainte-Anne - 138 route de Draguignan - Grasse; moulin Lotier - 102 av. des Acacias - Menton; moulin Alziari - 318 bd de la Madeleine - Nice. Lastly, above Aix-en-Provence, on the main road to Manosque in the Alpes-de-Haute-Provence, is another oil mill worth visiting: Moulin des Pénitents, les Mées (04 92 34 07 67).

The districts of Callas, Flayosc and Bargemon in the Var produce one of the best oils in the region. If you are heading for Salon, stop off at the Mas des Bories, veille route de Pelissane (Tel. 04 90 56 11 95), where you will find not only high quality oil but also *olives cassées*, delicious black olives and home made *tapenade*.

At the community oil press in L'Escarène (19, bd du Docteur-Roux), visitors can watch the traditional production of first pressed olive oil. The oil is sold in the neighbouring shops.

For holy liqueurs:

The liqueurs produced by the monks at Saint Honorat are sold in the monastery shop. Tel. 04 92 99 54 00.

OUTDOOR CAFÉS AND RESTAURANTS

Chez Bruno on the island of Sainte Marguerite (Cannes) serves fresh fish by the sea or in the shade under the pine trees. Tel. 04 93 43 49 30

Enjoy a quick lunch at the end of the Antibes market in the shade of an old southern nettle tree. La Croustille, 4 Cours Massena.

And for a nostalgic touch, enjoy a glass of pastis, served on a terrace shaded by plane trees, whilst listening to the sound of *pétanque*. To be avoided in August and on Sundays, but to be enjoyed with moderation as soon as the first warm rays of sunshine strike. Le Café de la Place, Saint-Paul.

At the Cala Blu, an excellent fish restaurant, the shimmering sea is within arm's reach. If you wanted to get any closer to the waves, you would need a pair of flippers and a floating table! Saint-Jean-Cap-Ferrat port. Tel 04 93 76 01 66.

Pottery, jams and all things nice

At the Nérolium farming cooperative, 12 av Georges Clemenceau in Vallauris, excellent citrus jams and little fragrant gifts. There are two addresses of note for pottery in Vallauris: Galerie Madoura, rue Suzanne-et-Georges-Ramié, and Sassi Milici, 65 bis rue Georges Clemenceau.

L'Herbier de Provence, descente de la Castre, Saint Paul: L'Occitane soaps, fragrances and bath products, as well as honey and good local olive oils.

Yvette Boselli Osteng in Tourrettes-sur-Loup, Tel. 04 93 59 28 44, sells the most magnificent violets from October to the end of March.

Confiserie Florian, Pont du Loup, Tourrettes-sur-Loup: crystallised fruit, fruit paste, home made jams, especially their jasmine, violet and rose jams. Food for angels or fairies!

Poterie Provençale, route de la Mer, Biot: a family business with lots of pretty things.

La Verrerie de Biot, 5 chemin des Combes: glassworks for all budgets and tastes, and especially good taste.

The Provençal market in Antibes: you'll find plenty of attractive pottery and other craftwork. And at 25 bis Cours Massena, a delicious selection of oils, jams and mustard.

Good socca?

Pipo Socca, 13 rue Bavastro, Nice: located just behind the port church. "Finger licking" socca! Some say it's the best ever.

A good fish market?

Every morning at Villefranche sur Mer, just above the church. The fish is still quivering, not just freshly fished that day, but that very hour.

An interesting flea market?

In front of the Saint-Pierre chapel in Villefranche-sur-Mer every Sunday from 10 am to 5 pm.

Some beautiful museums:

The Maeght Foundation, 623 chemin des Gardettes, Saint-Paul. Tel. 04 93 32 81 63. Amazing white concrete and red brick architecture by José Louis Sert. An excellent collection of works by leading names in contemporary art.

Musée Fernand Léger, chemin du Val de Pome, Biot. 340 of the artist's works, donated to the State by his wife.

Musée Renoir, chemin des Collettes, Cagnes-sur-Mer. The museum is in the Collettes estate, where Auguste Renoir spent the final years of his life. Beautiful canvases, fascinating studio and exquisite gardens.

Musée Marc Chagall, 7 avenue du Docteur Ménard, Nice. The largest collection of Chagall's works, a total of 400 oil paintings, gouaches and drawings.

Musée Matisse, 164 avenue des Arènes de Cimiez, Nice. A permanent collection donated by the painter and exhibited in an attractive red Italian style villa.

The Jules Chéret Museum of Fine Arts, 33 avenue des Baumettes, Nice. In an old townhouse which once belonged to a Russian princess. Interesting collection, including Monet, Fragonard, Dufy...

The "ancient" Greek villa Kerylos, in an exceptional location, almost too beautiful to be true. It is hard to understand how or why the villa came to exist here - the only explanation is for the sheer beauty of it. Rue Gustave Eiffel, Beaulieu-sur-Mer.

Legendary hotels

Le Yaca, Saint Tropez. Pretty rooms, a swimming pool surrounded by trees, a few tables outside... This is a pocket sized palace in the very centre of Saint-Trop'. Chic and charming, a little on the expensive side of course, but one should never hold back when in Saint-Tropez! 1 bd d'Aumale, Saint Tropez. Tel. 04 94 55 81 00.

Welcome Hotel, Villefranche-sur-Mer. Not exactly beautiful, a little too modernised for our taste, and they hardly have time to take your reservation...but this hotel is recommended simply because everybody who is anybody has stayed here. Not too bad, and perhaps even better off season, with pretty views all the same. 1, quai Amiral Courbet, Villefranche-sur-mer. Tel 04 93 76 27 62 (restaurant).

La Messardière, a peaceful and dreamlike location, surrounded by green gardens and blue skies, and just a stone's throw away from the sea, which is so close you can practically hear it breathing... And yet this hotel is located right in the thriving heart of legendary Saint Tropez. It's would be hard to imagine a better location for this celebrity residence. Even if you can't afford it, once, just once, would be worth it for a special occasion! This is the place to say that you'll love each other for ever, to promise yourselves everything and more. Even if it's not quite true and you've already done too much... isn't that right, Johnny? Domaine de la Messardière, route de Tahiti. Tel. 04 94 56 76 00.

CONTENTS

Introduction	9
The myth of the French Riviera	11
Menton	13
Monaco	16
Cap d'Ail	18
Beaulieu	18
Villefranche	19
Saint-Jean-Cap-Ferrat	20
Nice	22
Antibes	26
Le Cap d'Antibes	27
Juan-les-Pins	28
Cannes	29
Saint-Tropez	30
Discovering the Riviera's gardens	33
The medieval garden of Sainte-Agnès	35
The Val Rahmeh botanical gardens	35
Fontana Rosa gardens - Jardin des romanciers	36
Gardens of the Villa Maria Serena	36
The "Serre de la Madone" gardens	36
Japanese garden	38
The Fonvieille landscaped gardens and the Princess Grace rose garden	39
Jardin exotique de Monaco	40
Exotic garden of Eze	41
Kerylos Villa and gardens	42
Gardens and Villa Epherussi de Rothschild	44
The finest gardens in Nice	46
The Auguste-Renoir museum and gardens	48
Bonsai Arboretum	48
Etang de Fontmerle-Mougins	49
Botanical gardens of the Villa Thuret	49
Parc Explora	50
Ile Sainte-Marguerite	50
The Rayol Gardens	51
Tastes, scents and products of the Riviera	53
Pastis	54
The olive tree	55
Herbs	56
Basil	56
Rosemary	58
Bay leaves	58
Thyme	58
Sage	58
Chives	58

Marjoram or oregano	59
Wild thyme	59
Specialities of the sea	59
Wines	61
Fruits and flowers, tastes and scents	62
Tourettes-sur-Loup: food for the fairies	62
Eze: concentrated happiness	62
Traditional markets	64
Nice	65

Perched villages — 69

Gorbio	70
Sainte-Agnès	72
Roquebrune	74
Peille	74
Peillon	76
La Turbie	77
Eze	78
Saint-Paul	80
Vence	82
Tourettes-sur-Loup	82
Gourdon	84
Biot	86
Mougins	88
Ramatuelle	89
Gassin	90
Grimaud	90
Bormes-les-Mimosas	92

The islands — 97

ILES DE LÉRINS	97
Sainte-Marguerite: a delightful island	99
Saint-Honorat: the house of God	100
ILES D'HYÈRES, THE GOLDEN ISLANDS	106
The island of Porquerolles	107
Pors-Cros, treasure island	113
The Ile du Levant, the island of birds	118

Bibliography — 121
Recommended addresses — 123

More, much more than just a formal thank you to:
Air Liberté, which truly deserves its name.
Annie Meunier, and the dreamlike hotels she represents.
Mr Thierry Naidu, manager of the Château de la Chèvre d'Or

and also to:
René, for such unfailing support.
Stefano, with whom I can rest and recover.

Graphic design: Hokus Pokus
Map: Patrick Mérienne
Photogravure Nord Compo Villeneuve d'Ascq (59)
© 2001 - Edilarge S.A. - Editions Ouest-France

Cet ouvrage a été achevé d'imprimer par l'imprimerie Pollina à Luçon (85) - n° L83640
I.S.B.N. 2.7373.2811.X - Dépôt légal : Mai 2001
N° d'éditeur : 4187.01.03.05.01